Slim Buttes, 1876

Slim Buttes, 1876
An Episode of the Great Sioux War

by
JEROME A. GREENE

UNIVERSITY OF OKLAHOMA PRESS : NORMAN AND LONDON

By Jerome A. Greene

Evidence and the Custer Enigma (Kansas City, 1973)
Slim Buttes, 1876: An Episode of the Great Sioux War
  (Norman, 1982)

Library of Congress Cataloging-in-Publication Data

Greene, Jerome A.
  Slim Buttes, 1876.

  Bibliography: p. 179.
  Includes index.
  1. Slim Buttes (S.D.) Battle of, 1876.   I. Title.
E83.876.G74   973.8'2   81–40291
                                 AACR2
ISBN: 0–8061–2261–7

Dedicated to my parents,
Eben Gaynor Greene and
Dorothy Edgers Greene

CONTENTS

ILLUSTRATIONS

MAPS

PREFACE

IN ITS SHOCKING IMPACT, the news event of the year 1876 was the defeat and death at the hands of Indians of Lieutenant Colonel George A. Custer and five companies of the Seventh United States Cavalry at the Little Big Horn River. The unbelievable event of June 25, eclipsing all else that centennial summer, transpired in remote Montana Territory, a land most Americans could only imagine as a barren frontier inhabited by savages. So shocking was the catastrophe that people subsequently tended to forget that Little Big Horn was but the most memorable encounter in a long, frustrating military campaign to subjugate dissident groups of Teton Sioux and Northern Cheyenne Indians who refused to remain on their assigned reservation.

Little Big Horn symbolized the high-water mark of Sioux-Cheyenne predominance on the northern Great Plains. While that engagement represented the military zenith of those tribes, the Battle of Slim Buttes, which occurred on the rugged plains of Dakota scarcely eleven weeks later, signaled the waning of their fortunes. Indeed, Slim Buttes marked the first army triumph of the many sequential episodes collectively known as the Sioux War. For the Indians who gloried in the victory of Little Big Horn, Slim Buttes heralded the retaliatory blows that ultimately broke their resistance and forced their submission. The battle was the climax of the campaign of Brigadier General George Crook, perhaps the army's ablest Indian fighter, who led one of the most arduous military expeditions in American history. Crook's "starvation march," during which his soldiers were forced to subsist on horsemeat, was also extremely brutal in its punishment of some of the Indians who overwhelmed Custer. Tactically Slim Buttes epitomized the worst excesses of army-Indian warfare of the period. At the same time, for the soldiers, it was a significant, morale-raising encounter, involving one of the largest field commands to face Indian warriors in combat during the late nineteenth century. Most important from the standpoint of the army, however, the actions of September 9 and 10, 1876, commenced the relentless punitive warfare that was to be waged over the next eight months, until the tribesmen either had died or had gone peaceably to the agencies.

I first visited the Slim Buttes battlefield during Easter vacation, 1969, when I was a graduate student in the University of South Dakota, Vermillion. It was a memorable experience. I met Ralph E. Waugh, a ninety-five-year-old retired rancher who had homesteaded near the Buttes in 1909. As a lad Waugh, reared in Rapid City, had known Annie Tallent, "Calamity Jane" Cannary and other early Black Hills notables. A charming, observant, and extraordinarily sensitive man, he expressed considerable sympathy for the Indians who once ranged over his property. He had been present at the celebration marking the erection of the Slim Buttes battle marker in 1920, and now, forty-nine years later, he kindly accompanied me over the field, in a strenuous exercise for one his age, and pointed out to me the places where he believed significant action had occurred. On subsequent visits to Slim Buttes, I always stopped by to see Waugh. He died in 1973.

In July, 1975, my wife and I spent a week camping at Slim Buttes. We trekked for miles across the rugged ground, armed with books, cameras, and topographic maps, as we sought to ascertain how the battle had unfolded. Because no coherent map of troop movement during the battle had been found, our task was to determine locations where prolonged firing had occurred and relate them to the several eyewitness accounts of the engagement that we possessed. Much of the present book encompasses the results of that work.

The land on which Slim Buttes battlefield is situated belongs to George Lermeny, of Reva, South Dakota. I am grateful to Lermeny for recognizing the importance of our terrain survey to a complete understanding of the battle and for permitting us access to his property. Others who assisted in this endeavor and who contributed to make this book possible include Nancy O. Klock, Manchester, Connecticut, the granddaughter of Captain Anson Mills, who led the assault on the Indian village in 1876; Mark H. Brown, Alta, Iowa; B. William Henry, Jr., Fort Larned National Historic Site, Kansas; Merrill J. Mattes, Littleton, Colorado; A. Berle Clemensen, National Park Service, Denver, Colorado; L. Clifford Soubier, National Park Service, Harpers Ferry, West Virginia; Erwin N. Thompson, National Park Service, Denver, Colorado; William A. Dobak, Newberry Library, Chicago; Paul L. Hedren, Golden Spike National Historic Site, Utah; Don Rickey, Jr., Bureau of Land Management, Denver; Myrle G. Hanson, Spearfish, South Dakota; Robert and Frieda Elling, Reva, South Dakota; and David B. Miller, Sever L. Eubank, Michael Jackley, and Paul Haivala, Black Hills State College, Spearfish, South Dakota.

Public repositories and institutions that aided me in my work include: South Dakota State Historical Society, Pierre; Butte County Historical Society, Newell, South Dakota; W. H. Over Museum, University of South Dakota, Vermillion; Fort Laramie National Historic Site, Wyoming; Lilly Library, University of Indiana, Bloomington; Western History Collections, University of Colorado Library, Boulder; Nebraska State Historical Society, Lincoln; Wyoming

State Historical Society, Cheyenne; United States Army Military History Institute, Carlisle Barracks, Pennsylvania; National Archives, Washington, D.C.; Library of Congress, Washington, D.C.; Western History Division, Denver Public Library; Western History Research Center, University of Wyoming Library, Laramie; Custer Battlefield National Monument, Montana; Manuscript Division, Brigham Young University Library, Provo, Utah; Western History Collections, University of Oklahoma Library, Norman; and University of Kansas Library, Lawrence.

Finally, I thank my wife, Linda, for her help. Without her valuable assistance this book could not have been possible.

JEROME A. GREENE

Denver, Colorado

Slim Buttes, 1876

I may claim here that the little handful of men that makes up our Regular Army is entitled to some praise for having been the pioneers in wresting step by step, foot by foot, from the savage, an Empire beyond the Missouri, vast in area, boundless in resources, which shall be a heritage to your children and your children's children forever.

George Crook, address at the reunion of the Army of West Virginia, 1884.

Then followed the memorable campaign of 1876. . . . We set out with ten days' rations on a chase that lasted ten weeks. We roamed some eighteen hundred miles over range and prairie, over "bad lands" and worse waters. We wore out some Indians, a good many soldiers, and a great many horses. We sometimes caught the Indians, and sometimes they caught us. It was hot, dry summer weather when we left our wagons, tents, and extra clothing; it was sharp and freezing before we saw them again. . . . Never, I venture to say, never was civilized army in such a plight as was the command of General George Crook when his brigade of regulars halted on the north bank of the Belle Fourche in September, 1876.

Charles King, "Van," *Starlight Ranch and Other Stories of Army Life on the Frontier,* 1890.

Chapter 1
The Big Horn
and
Yellowstone Expedition

THE THREE SOLDIERS SAT THEIR HORSES and peered anxiously at the sight before them. It was early Wednesday morning, July 12, 1876, and miles away across the broken, pine-speckled hills of northern Wyoming they could see the vague forms of several hundred pitched tents. The haze of smoldering prairie fires filled the morning air, however, and they were unsure whether the tents belonged to army troops or to Indians. Cautiously the men pushed forward, aware of the urgency of the message they bore. As they drew closer, clouds of smoke billowed ahead, obscuring the tents from view. The men drove on persistently. An hour later they dashed their mounts through the crackling underbrush and presented themselves at the camp of Brigadier General George Crook, United States Army.

For their gallantry in carrying vital dispatches through country teeming with hostile Indians, the army later awarded Medals of Honor to Privates William Evans, Benjamin F. Stewart, and James Bell, all of Company E, Seventh Infantry. They had journeyed for three days from the Yellowstone River camp of Brigadier General Alfred H. Terry to reach Crook's headquarters, known as Camp Cloud Peak, along Big Goose Creek near present-day Sheridan, Wyoming.[1] The important news they carried was the defeat and destruction on June 25 of Lieutenant Colonel George A. Custer and five companies of the Seventh Cavalry in a battle sixty miles north, along the Little Big Horn

3

River. The information was already two days old among Crook's soldiers; they had learned of the Custer disaster from dispatches arriving from the south. But the grisly details furnished by troops who had actually been on the scene and helped bury the dead lent immediacy to the event.

The defeat of Custer held special meaning for Crook's men, for it had occurred only eight days after their own besting by many of these same Indians in a fierce, day-long encounter on the upper reaches of Rosebud Creek. Crook's northward offensive had been checked at the Rosebud, and he had returned south to his present position, thereby failing to make an anticipated union with Terry's command in the Yellowstone country. The Custer disaster contained an obvious negative implication for Crook personally: had he—despite his setback at the Rosebud—continued north with his thousand-man contingent and joined Terry in time, the Little Big Horn catastrophe might well have been averted.

Yet all this seemed typical of the moment. For Crook the Sioux Campaign of 1876 had been thus far a frustrating exercise. In March the military operations to force the dissident elements of the Teton Dakota Indians—commonly referred to as Sioux—back onto their reservation in southwestern Dakota Territory had begun in earnest. The "hostiles," as the government officially designated these Indians, comprised representatives of all the Teton tribes: Hunkpapas, Oglalas, Minneconjous, Brulés, Two Kettles, Sans Arcs, and Blackfeet. After the tribesmen spurned a federal ultimatum to go to their assigned agencies, the War Department sent troops to force their compliance.

The first to take the field of three army columns closing on the Yellowstone–Big Horn rivers region of Montana from the east, west, and south, Crook's force had experienced more than its share of battle at the hands of the Indi-

Brigadier General George Crook, attired in a private soldier's overcoat, his typical campaign garb. Courtesy of the Custer Battlefield National Monument, Crow Agency, Montana.

ans. The first major contact occurred on March 17, when soldiers commanded by Colonel Joseph J. Reynolds fell upon a village on the Powder River in southeastern Montana Territory. Reynolds drove out most of the inhabitants, captured a large pony herd, and burned the tipis. Yet the Indians resisted fiercely, despite subzero temperatures, and after a five-hour struggle Reynolds lost the initiative and permitted the tribesmen to retrieve their horses. News of the failure angered Crook, and his charges forced Reynolds's court-martial and subsequent resignation from the service. Significantly, the troops had struck a peaceful camp of Northern Cheyennes instead of Sioux. Thereafter those Indians became active belligerents in the Sioux War.[2]

The Powder River fight was a reversal for the army. Reynolds burned valuable provisions on which Crook had hoped to subsist his troops, and the loss forced him to withdraw his soldiers from the region until late spring. At that time Crook again proceeded north, but on June 17, along Montana's Rosebud, his troops were again foiled by the Sioux and Cheyennes.[3] After his withdrawal to Goose Creek to regroup and await reinforcements, these Indians united to destroy Custer.

Custer's fall came when he tried to surprise an encampment of Indians thirty miles northwest of the Rosebud battle site. His Seventh Cavalry regiment was a major component of General Terry's eastern contingent from Fort Abraham Lincoln, Dakota. The Fort Lincoln column was to work harmoniously with Crook's and with another column from Fort Shaw and Fort Ellis in Montana commanded by Colonel John Gibbon. To that end Custer was sent to reconnoiter the Rosebud and to cooperate with Gibbon in enveloping an Indian village suspected to be in Little Big Horn Valley. Unaware of Crook's retirement from the field, Custer ascended the Rosebud and headed west toward the Little Big Horn. Fearful that the tribesmen had learned of his presence, he dropped plans for a concerted strike at dawn on June 26 and advanced immediately, a day early. Custer's bold attack on the village at midday miscarried tragically.[4]

News of this third and most resounding military defeat of the Sioux War fell like a thunderbolt among Crook and his men and created disheartening morale problems for all the troops left in the field, who would be expected to avenge the losses. For the moment Crook decided to stay at his present position and await further word of the military situation and the anticipated reinforcements.

Oddly enough, despite his close proximity to Custer's battleground, Crook did not get word of the encounter until almost a week after the American public read of it in the newspapers. Across the nation the reaction was one of dismay. In the West editors called for a speedy "prosecution of the war in a manner so vigorous that the fiends of the plains will be glad to surrender their arms." The hostiles should be "exterminated root and branch, old and young, male and female."[5] Eastern papers also expressed alarm but mirrored geographical detachment and humanitarian tendencies in their more subdued urgency. "We must beat the Sioux," opined a *New York Times* editorial, "but we need not exterminate them."[6]

For the army in the wake of Little Big Horn neither remedy appeared imminent. After three defeats in as many months the Sioux campaign stood in danger of foundering. Lieutenant General Philip H. Sheridan, commanding the Military Division of the Missouri from his headquarters in Chicago, worked assiduously to formulate a new strategy and to gather replacements for Custer's dead. Two military departments in Sheridan's division constituted the focal point for the field maneuvers: the Department of Dakota, under Terry, included both Dakota and Montana territories, while Crook's Department of the Platte included Nebraska and all of Wyoming Territory. Troops were needed to augment the forces of each of these field commanders. The

government acted swiftly; the manpower problem was
partly resolved early in August with passage by Congress of
a bill increasing the cavalry arm by 2,500 men.[7]

Recruitment of auxiliary soldiers took time, however,
and for the present the army was left to manage as it could
with the resources available. Troops far removed from the
Sioux conflict suddenly found themselves active partici-
pants as telegraphed orders sent them into the field. Ten
companies of the Fifth Cavalry stationed along the Kansas
Pacific Railroad received orders to proceed by train to
Cheyenne, Wyoming, and then march overland to join
Crook's command. Detachments of the Fourth, Ninth, and
Fourteenth Infantries also proceeded north to Crook. From
Fort Leavenworth, Kansas, and the Indian Territory (Okla-
homa) came the Fifth Infantry under Colonel Nelson A.
Miles to reinforce Terry on the Yellowstone.[8] The arrival of
these men took time, and the armies of Crook and Terry
waited impatiently to resume maneuvers.

While occupying himself primarily with increasing troop
strength and planning their movements, General Sheridan
also urged a swift military takeover of the Sioux agencies in
Dakota and northwest Nebraska, a precautionary measure
designed to keep heretofore peaceful tribesmen at those locations from joining the hostiles as well as to prevent the
hostiles from coming to the agencies while they remained
troublesome. The Department of the Interior acquiesced
to Sheridan's urging; as of late July, and until otherwise de-
creed, civil officials became subordinate to army officers
appointed to the agencies. Tribesmen living at the Red
Cloud and Spotted Tail agencies in Nebraska and at the
Standing Rock and Cheyenne River agencies in Dakota
were to be relieved of their guns and horses.[9] Moreover,
instructed Sheridan, "on no account will any Indians be allowed to return to the Agencies without unconditional surrender of their persons, ponies, guns and ammunition."[10]
To ensure sufficient military strength throughout the Great

Sioux Reservation, the general ordered the entire Eleventh Infantry north from Texas, and half the Fourth Cavalry under Colonel Ranald S. Mackenzie from the Indian Territory, Kansas, and Texas. Units of the First, Second, Third, and Fourth Artilleries were sent from both coasts to occupy forts in Sheridan's division now vacated by the troops normally stationed in them.[11]

Even as Sheridan implemented his plans for the agencies, trouble flared. On July 15 several hundred Cheyennes fled the Red Cloud Agency in Nebraska in an effort to join the hostiles in northern Wyoming. Colonel Wesley Merritt, en route to meet Crook with seven companies of the Fifth Cavalry, fortuitously intercepted the tribesmen two days later and forced them back to the agency. One Indian warrior was killed and one wounded in the skirmish at Hat, or Warbonnet, Creek in extreme northwestern Nebraska. By sanction of the Interior Department, Red Cloud Agency thereafter became a veritable armed post under the watchful eyes of Mackenzie's Fourth Cavalry at nearby Camp Robinson.[12] With the other agencies similarly managed, army efforts turned once more to actively subduing the hostiles and ending the Sioux War.

In the meantime, after their victory on the Little Big Horn the combined Sioux and Northern Cheyenne force, numbering about 15,000 men, women, and children, drifted south to the Big Horn Mountains, their traditional summer hunting grounds. Adhering to established seasonal peregrinations, the tribesmen in late July began migrating north and east toward Dakota Territory. They passed the site of their recent success against Custer, moved over to Rosebud Creek, where they camped for a while, and then continued east toward the Tongue and Powder rivers. As they moved, the Indians fired the grass and underbrush for miles about, and until well into August the area between the Big Horn and Powder rivers was a smoky, blackened wasteland. The burning was meant not so much to hinder

Principal engagements of the Sioux War, 1876–77, and General Crook's route from Camp Cloud Peak to the Black Hills in August and September, 1876.

army movements as to bring forth young grass early the next spring, when the tribesmen fully expected to hunt the region again.[13]

When the hostiles reached Powder River, they began to fragment. Economic reality dictated a breakup if the Indians were to survive on the existing game. At the mouth of Blue Stone Creek the major division occurred; some Indians went north toward the Yellowstone River, while others traveled south up the Powder. Most of the tribesmen headed east in small bands toward the Little Missouri River.

The eastward migrants included Indians bound for the popular Bear Butte trade point, east of the northern Black Hills in Dakota. Most of these people sought guns and ammunition with which to fight the soldiers and prolong their independence. Others were going to the agencies, where they hoped to receive sustenance until early spring, when they too could resume their unfettered existence.[14]

The new military posture at the agencies dashed all such plans. Those warriors who unwittingly entered an agency were to be quickly dismounted and disarmed.[15] "A Sioux on foot," philosophized General Sheridan, "is a Sioux warrior no longer."[16] Even rumors of the impending surrender of no less an antagonist than the Oglala leader Crazy Horse left Sheridan unswayed. "He wants now to shake hands and make peace," said one report. Said the general, "I expect to shake him a little myself before the peace is concluded."[17]

General Crook's command, which had been bivouacked at Goose Creek since its withdrawal from the Rosebud in June, received its first reinforcements on July 11, when more than 200 Ute and Shoshoni scouts arrived under the army's old ally Chief Washakie. Crook expected more soldiers, however. He had known for some time that the Fifth Cavalry had taken the field, and the latest word from Sheridan indicated how Crook might use these troops when they arrived. On the advice of Commanding General William T. Sherman, Sheridan suggested that Crook combine forces with Terry, and Terry's own dispatches, received at the Goose Creek camp on July 12, urged the same course. Crook agreed, but he determined to await the arrival of the Fifth Cavalry before resuming the campaign, and he sent word to Colonel Merritt to join him immediately at Camp Cloud Peak.[18]

Sheridan too preferred that Crook await reinforcements before renewing operations, and while Crook passed the time reconnoitering the countryside, his men, who had none too humorously dubbed him "Rosebud George," remained critical of the delay, despite the holding orders from Chicago.[19] Some troopers condemned Crook's management of the campaign, calling it irresponsible to permit "the Indians to withdraw from his front without any knowledge of the time they had left."[20] As debate over his inaction swirled in the ranks, Crook's force was augmented further with the arrival on July 13 of seven companies of infantry troops and a supply train. Three days later Crook responded to Terry's letter, agreeing to meet him after Merritt's cavalry had arrived. He suggested that perhaps Terry might begin gradually moving in Crook's direction so as to help provide mutual security for the commands.[21] Crook was unaware of Merritt's action on the Warbonnet on July 17, which delayed Merritt's juncture with the army column on Goose Creek.

Weeks passed uneventfully as Crook fretted over Merritt's whereabouts. Eager to start north, Crook sent his scouts, Indian and white, to check the surrounding country for signs of Indians. One party of Shoshonis under Washakie searched the headwaters of the Little Big Horn and reported that the hostiles had moved away from the area. They were evidently hungry and had left in quest of game, for Washakie's scouts found hundreds of dog and pony bones scattered about the abandoned campgrounds.[22]

On August 1, his patience exhausted, Crook moved his command a short distance over the fire-blackened terrain to Tongue River, hoping to get some inkling of either Terry's or the Indians' presence. Terry was nowhere to be found, and it was evident that the hostiles had indeed departed for fresh hunting grounds. On August 2 couriers from Merritt reached Crook announcing that the Fifth Cavalry troops were now moving up Goose Creek. The next day Crook set his command marching to meet the tardy column. The forces of Crook and Merritt finally united in the evening of August 3.[23]

The Fifth Cavalry, which had formerly served Crook in Arizona, contributed ten companies to his command, along with seventy-six fresh recruits conducted north by Merritt's soldiers.[24] The following day, August 4, Crook announced the organization of the Big Horn and Yellowstone Expedition. All the cavalry units—ten companies of the Fifth, five of the Second, and ten of the Third—formed a cavalry brigade composed of four battalions headed by Colonel Merritt. The Fifth Cavalry Regiment was placed under Lieutenant Colonel Eugene A. Carr. Major John J. Upham commanded the first battalion of the Fifth, Major Julius W. Mason the second. The combined units of the Second and Third Cavalries were commanded by Lieutenant Colonel William B. Royall. Under Royall was a Second Cavalry battalion commanded by Captain Henry E. Noyes and a Third Cavalry battalion under Major Andrew W. Evans.

In addition to the cavalry, ten companies of infantry— three of the Fourth, three of the Ninth, and four of the Fourteenth—were formed into a unified provisional regiment headed by Major Alexander Chambers of the Fourth. Captain George M. Randall, attached from the Twenty-third Infantry, was placed in charge of the 240 Indian scouts, while Major Thaddeus H. Stanton, paymaster, commanded all irregulars and civilian employees, includ-

Colonel Wesley Merritt of the Fifth Cavalry, who commanded Crook's cavalry brigade in the 1876 campaign and was superintendent of the Military Academy at West Point during the early 1880s, when this picture was taken. Courtesy of the Western History Collections, University of Colorado Library, Boulder.

ing 44 white volunteer scouts and guides. Eight medical personnel attached to the headquarters staff accompanied the column under the command of the expedition's medical director, Dr. Bennett A. Clements. The press was represented by several correspondents, four of whom had earlier been with Crook to report on the Rosebud encounter. Irish-born John F. Finerty chronicled the army's daily activities for the *Chicago Times*, while Reuben Briggs Davenport represented the *New York Herald*, Robert E. Strahorn the *Rocky Mountain News* (Denver) and *The Chicago Tribune*, and Joe Wasson the *New York Tribune* and *Alta California* (San Francisco). Other correspondents arrived with Merritt's column. In all the Big Horn and Yellowstone Expedition numbered about 2,200 men, including nearly 1,500 cavalry, 450 infantry, and the various scouts.[25]

Several members of the expedition deserve more than passing notice. Chief among them was General Crook, who was forty-seven years old and was looked upon as a preeminent field officer and Indian fighter. An 1852 graduate of West Point, the gray-eyed, bearded Crook had spent several years fighting Indians in the Northwest and had received a painful arrow wound during the Rogue River War in Oregon. During the Civil War he had risen to the rank of major general of volunteers and had conducted many important military operations for the Union. He had fought at Winchester, Fishers Hill, and Cedar Creek, Virginia and elsewhere, and had played a major role in the campaign leading to Appomattox in 1865. After the war Crook returned to the West and resumed Indian campaigning. He led troops against the truculent Apaches in the Southwest, and in 1873 he was made a brigadier general in the regular army. In the spring of 1875 Crook was appointed commander of the Military Department of the Platte with headquarters at Omaha.

A man of medium size, Crook possessed a sharp nose and

Major Alexander Chambers of the Fourth Infantry, a brigadier general of volunteers during the Civil War, who commanded the infantry brigade under Crook in 1876. Courtesy of the U.S. Military Academy Archives, West Point, New York.

an angular jaw that spoke of stubborn determination. He abhorred military etiquette and in the field wore the plain clothes of an ordinary private soldier. He disdained pretension and often could be seen on campaign plodding along astride a mule, his long reddish beard braided and tied. An item in a California paper during the Apache troubles of the early 1870s spoke of him in these terms:

The fact is, Crook is nothing but an Indian. . . . I mean that his mind, physiognomy and education are all Indian. Look at his face, . . . [the] high cheek bones [and] the contour of his skull; and his manners—stolid, separate, averse to talk. He can take his gun and cross the desert, subsisting on the way where you or I would starve. Perfectly self-reliant for any venture, delighted with lonely travel and personal hazard, carrying nothing but his arms, he will walk after a trail all day and when night comes, no matter how cold, he wraps himself in an Indian blanket, humped up, Indian fashion, and pitches himself into a sage brush, there to be perfectly easy till morning. He will follow an antelope for three days. He requires nothing to drink or smoke, and very little to eat. Abstemious, singular [sic] utterly ignorant of fear, and yet stealthy as a cat, shy of women and strangers; and when he was a cadet he had all the same traits.[26]

Before this campaign Crook had had no experience fighting the Sioux and Cheyennes. The abortive fight at Rosebud Creek on June 17—which Crook stubbornly insisted on calling a victory—convinced him that this new enemy could be fully as unyielding as he was.

The second-ranking man with the Big Horn and Yellowstone Expedition was Wesley Merritt, the young colonel commanding Crook's cavalry brigade. Merritt, who had just turned forty in June, fairly typified the aggressive cavalry officers that army superiors wanted in the field. He had been, in fact, a Civil War contemporary of Custer's, operating under Sheridan as a brigadier general in many of the campaigns of the Army of the Potomac. Merritt had served at Gettysburg, Yellow Tavern, and Five Forks, had led a cavalry division during the Shenandoah Campaign, and had commanded an entire corps at Appomattox. Since 1865 the handsome, round-faced, somewhat contentious officer had served mostly with the all-black Ninth Cavalry.[27] As of July 1, 1876, he commanded the Fifth Cavalry, an appointment that nettled the man whose place he had appropriated, Lieutenant Colonel Eugene A. Carr.

Carr was forty-six years old in the summer of 1876. He was an old-timer, a proven Indian fighter. Nicknamed "War Eagle," Carr had served in Texas and New Mexico during the 1850s and during the Civil War had campaigned in the Middle West and South. He had fought in Missouri, Tennessee, Arkansas, and Mississippi, becoming a brigadier general of volunteers in 1862. After the war Carr again fought Indians and won a deserved reputation as a hardbitten cavalry commander and an ardent battlefield foe of the Sioux and Cheyennes. A Medal of Honor winner for his Civil War performance at Wilson's Creek, Missouri, Carr had also acquired a cranky disposition and a seemingly contemptuous attitude toward his immediate superiors. Thus Merritt's appointment to command the Fifth annoyed the older officer greatly.[28]

Among other noteworthy persons assembled at Goose Creek was Crook's designated head scout, Frank Grouard. The skillful frontiersman, only twenty-five years old in 1876, was alleged to have been born in the South Pacific, the son of an American missionary and his Polynesian wife (another story was that he was the son of a Creole man and an Oglala Sioux woman). As a youth Grouard had been captured by a party of Sioux while working as a mail rider in Montana. Supposedly saved from death by his swarthy complexion, he spent several years with his captors, learning their language and lifeways and becoming knowledgeable about the country they inhabited. The experience served him well; after he left the Sioux, Grouard took employment with the army and rose quickly in General

Lieutenant Colonel Eugene A. Carr, an experienced Indian fighter, who commanded the Fifth Cavalry at Slim Buttes. Courtesy of the National Archives, Washington, D.C.

Crook's esteem. Possessed of a penchant for exaggerating his self-importance, however, in addition to an apparent timidity in crises, Grouard would emerge from the summer campaign an enigmatic personality of dubious over-all value to his employers.

Technically relegated below Grouard in the hierarchy of civilian employees was the redoubtable William F. ("Buffalo Bill") Cody, who had forsaken the footlights of the East to scout for Merritt, doubtless to gain publicity to bolster his stage show. Cody had shown his sense of theatrical timing during the recent skirmish on the Warbonnet, when he had dispatched a young Cheyenne warrior named Yellow Hair, a feat heralded by eastern newspapers as the "First Scalp for Custer." An eyewitness to the encounter, who would one day describe it in classic Victorian prose, was First Lieutenant Charles King, an able observer who in the 1880s and 1890s became known to thousands as a writer of military novels. John Gregory Bourke, Crook's assistant adjutant general, was a man of similar literary merit as well as scientific bent who years later would graphically depict his experiences on the frontier serving under Crook.[29]

A great many of Crook's subalterns were seasoned Indian campaigners. Many were Civil War veterans with commendable records in combat. Some had served at lofty rank but at war's end had been relegated to lower status. Complementing them were younger officers, only lately graduated from the Military Academy or risen from the enlisted ranks. Not surprisingly, the presence of an assortment of strong older personalities would in time weigh on the expedition. Since the Powder River fight and the subsequent arrest of Colonel Reynolds in May there had existed a festering division of opinion in the command over Crook's handling of the affair. Petty jealousies arising between the senior officers of the Fifth Cavalry complicated the situation. By the end of the summer the discord, aggravated by the physical strain of the march, was coming to the surface

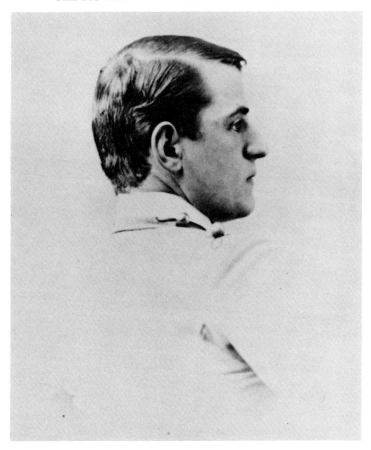

First Lieutenant John G. Bourke, an 1869 West Point graduate, who served as Crook's adjutant during the 1876 Sioux campaign. Courtesy of the U.S. Military Academy Archives.

frequently. Even the enlisted men became sensitive to the angry nuances floating around camp and reflected in their own comments the obvious dissension among the leaders. The ever-watchful press corps none too objectively took sides in the rift, and their dispatches sometimes connoted

First Lieutenant Charles King, regimental adjutant of the Fifth Cavalry. He suffered through the Crook campaign with an agonizing wound he had received during an Apache fight in the Southwest some years before. Forced to retire in 1879 because of the injury, King became a prolific writer on military subjects. He died in 1933. Courtesy of the U.S. Military Academy Archives.

pro- or anti-Crook biases. Reuben Davenport, of the *New-York Herald*, was particularly critical of the campaign management, while Finerty, Strahorn, and Wasson were generally supportive of Crook.[30]

Because he was late starting and because the hostiles had, in effect, stolen a march on him, Crook decided to proceed as rapidly as he could to try to overtake them. Rather than let it hinder his movement, he ordered the 160-wagon supply train to stay behind at Goose Creek, in the charge of Quartermaster John V. Furey. Helping Furey guard the provisions were two hundred teamsters and discharged soldiers who were awaiting escort to Fort Fetterman, sixty miles south. On the march Crook's troops would carry a bare minimum of rations and other necessities. They would take only enough hardtack, bacon, coffee, sugar, and salt to last fourteen days. By the expiration of that time the Yellowstone supply depot would have been reached. To travel lightly and rapidly, each soldier carried only essential gear—blanket, tin cup, frying pan, and eating utensils. No tents were permitted. Each soldier took four days' rations on his person. Extra rations, along with extra ammunition, went forward on the backs of 240 pack mules.[31]

The soldiers sported the uniforms and equipment prescribed by army regulations. Troopers of the Second and Third Cavalry appeared the most unkempt because they had been in the field longer than Merritt's men. All the men wore surplus fatigue clothing from Civil War stockpiles or the newer issue clothing adopted in 1872. The uniform consisted of a loose-fitting dark-blue woolen blouse fastened with four or five brass eagle buttons in front and baggy, sky-blue wool trousers held up with suspenders. Infantrymen wore leather shoes with soles affixed with brass screws; cavalrymen wore either the issue knee-high boots or privately purchased canvas puttees. Each soldier wore a broad-brimmed hat, the black, floppy style adopted in 1872 or one of felt or straw purchased from a sutler. Cavalry troopers were armed with the 1873 Model Colt single-action revolver and the 1873 Model Springfield Trapdoor carbine; infantry soldiers carried the same 1873 model but longer Springfield rifle. Cartridges were carried in hand-fashioned looped belts or in leather boxes specially issued for revolver and long-arms ammunition and worn on a waistbelt. Rations, clothing, and other accouterments were transported in slinged haversacks or saddlebags. Each soldier carried a wool-covered, pint-capacity tin canteen—a surplus article from the Civil War.[32]

Thus organized and provisioned, the expedition settled in for its last night at Goose Creek. As correspondent Finerty reported:

That night it blew great guns. It was our last chance under canvas for some time, and Old Boreas determined that we shouldn't enjoy it. Three-fourths of the tents were blown down, and so terrible were the clouds of dust and smoke blown from the burning prairies and wooded hills that suffocation was imminent with those who had the philosophy, or the necessary weariness, to sleep.[33]

That night was but a portent of things to come.

Chapter 2
To the Yellowstone

THE BIG HORN AND YELLOWSTONE EXPEDITION left camp on Saturday morning, August 5, and moved north. Stripped of all cumbersome equipment, the men marched off lightly "like the highwaymen of old," wrote Finerty.[1] The foot soldiers left Goose Creek at about four o'clock, three hours ahead of the cavalry, which remained to help bundle the tents and excess baggage to be left with Quartermaster Furey. Most of the Second and Third Cavalries—those soldiers who had been in the field constantly since winter—were tired and haggard. Their mounts had eaten no corn or grain for two months, "and at least a third of them looked well fitted for the bone yard."[2] Moreover, the horses of Merritt's regiment, which normally would have been fresh, were exhausted from the Warbonnet exercise and the subsequent race to the Red Cloud Agency, a movement that some critics said retarded Crook's advance until after the hostiles had left the Big Horn country.[3]

The cavalry advanced in three columns, preceded by a number of guides directed by Cody and Grouard. All day the command moved slowly north, passing along Prairie Dog Creek to Tongue River and past the site where hostile Sioux had fired on the encamped soldiers on June 9. After twenty miles the troops stopped for the night. As a precaution against surprise attack by the Indians, Crook placed his men in a large protective circle with all the livestock inside. The arrangement was continued on succeeding nights.[4]

Crook learned from Crow scouts previously sent him by
Terry that the hostiles' trail lay somewhere ahead. He
feared, however, that the Indians would ultimately scatter
to seek game rather than meet the soldiers in combat so
soon after the fight with Custer. Accordingly, the general
directed his column down the Tongue River, crossing it
no less than seventeen times on August 6. The command
traveled an estimated twenty-five miles that day in temperatures reckoned by some to be 105° F. The next day
the troops left the Tongue and marched west to Rosebud
Creek, striking that stream about ten miles below the battle site of June 17.[5]

On the morning of August 8 the soldiers awoke amid so
much fog and smoke that they could scarcely see their comrades. After a few hours of groping slowly along the Rosebud and investigating the site of an abandoned Indian village, Crook ordered a halt. In the late afternoon a breeze
cleared the air, and at six the march was resumed, continuing into the early-morning hours. A participant described the progression:

Not a sound was heard but the solemn tramp of the cavalry columns advancing through the gloom, except when a solitary jack-
ass, attached to the pack-train, gave vent to his perturbed feelings in a bray which, amid the mountain echoes, sounded like the
laughter of a legion of mocking devils.[6]

After promptly muzzling the offender, the column halted at
2:00 A.M. and went into bivouac.

On Wednesday, the fourth day out of Goose Creek,
Crook's army traveled slightly over twenty miles through
the still-smoldering country. This region of the Rosebud
held immense quantities of anthracite coal, and the recent
incendiary activities of the Sioux and Cheyennes had left
many outcroppings of the combustible substance slowly
burning. Correspondent Finerty likened Rosebud Valley to

"a huge coal bed—one of the most extensive in America." "Some day," he prophesied, "when the Sioux are all in the happy hunting grounds, this valley will rival the Lehigh of Pennsylvania."[7] That day two men arrived from Fort Fetterman with mail and dispatches for Crook. One was a Montana "volunteer," the other "Captain" Jack Crawford, the famous "poet scout" and theatrical colleague of Cody.[8] "Our camp fires were lively after Captain Jack joined us," recalled an officer. "He sang his songs, told his stories, recited his poems, and kept his tireless jaw constantly wagging for our edification."[9]

While Crook's column had been tracing its way toward the Yellowstone, hoping to gain knowledge of the Indians' whereabouts, General Terry had ascended the Rosebud, seeking to establish communication with Crook. On August 10, thirty miles above the mouth of the Rosebud, the columns fairly collided with each other in an embarrassing and somewhat comical surprise meeting. Cody had been sent to determine the source of a dust column rising in the north. He returned and reported that Terry was near, and Crook ordered his force to encamp. But Terry's scouts, frantic at seeing the Shoshonis in Crook's van, had dispatched word of hostiles to Terry, who deployed his troops into battle readiness and advanced before realizing the true identity of his adversaries.[10] With Terry's command rode the survivors of Custer's old regiment; their presence, so soon after the memorable defeat, made a deep impression on the soldiers with Crook. Wrote Finerty:

The principal thing that attracted my attention and that of all our force was the remnant of the 7th Cavalry. It came in, formed into eight small companies, led by Maj. Reno [Custer's second in command at Little Big Horn]—a short, stout man, about 50 years old,—with a determined visage, his face showing intimate acquaintance with the sun and wind. . . . Many of the officers and men looked tired, dirty, and disgusted.[11]

Crook too was privately disgusted. While he politely insisted that the senior-ranking Terry assume command of the two armies, he was dismayed and agitated by his situation. The command, he reportedly divulged to a friend, was too big and unwieldy to undertake an offensive against the Sioux. "We shall find no Indians while such a force sticks together," he said.[12] Despite the complexities now posed by size, the commands of Terry and Crook, under the nominal head of Terry, set out to find the tribesmen. Emulating Crook, Terry loaded all his extra provisions into his wagons and sent them under the escort of Colonel Nelson A. Miles to the mouth of the Rosebud. The day after their meeting the two armies, exceeding four thousand men, pushed eastward to the Tongue River, where the soldiers found and buried the skeleton of a miner who had been killed months before. In camp the men of the various units made new acquaintances, renewed old ones, and shared comments about the campaign's progress. The five companies of the Second Cavalry were at least temporarily reunited with the remainder of the regiment—those companies serving in Colonel John Gibbon's command under Terry. It was the first time in seven years that the regiment had marched together.[13]

During the night of the eleventh the weather turned rainy and blustery, and Crook's men, without tents, endured the storm with discomfort. "Inches in altitude were of far more importance than grades in rank," remembered Colonel Gibbon, "and happy was he who had . . . placed his blanket on an elevation and not in a depression."[14] Bad weather continued into the afternon of the twelfth, greatly impeding the advance. "All sleep in rain and dirt, drink coarse coffee, eat hardtack and chew raw bacon," reported Finerty. "All this is the concomitant of war and fame. The rays of the star of 'glory' are made up of filth, hardship, and disappointments."[15] "During the whole night the rain kept falling," wrote an officer of the Third Cavalry, "and the 'clerk of the weather,' as if to add insult to injury, gave us a bitter cold morning in which to enjoy our wet clothing." [16]

Nevertheless, the combined commands kept on in pursuit of the elusive and seemingly long-vanished foe. Cavalry horses, tired from weeks of campaigning, now began to play out, and some had to be abandoned. Even the mounts of the Fifth Cavalry, supposedly fresh in comparison with those of other units, had begun to collapse from exhaustion by the time the troops reached Pumpkin Creek and directed their march east toward Powder River. So worn out were the horses that Crook's infantrymen had gone into bivouac long before the equestrians reached camp. [17] On August 15 the columns arrived in Powder River Valley where they found numerous springs with fresh water, a pleasant contrast to "the water in the clay-bank creeks [that] had the consistency of thick cream." [18]

The next afternoon, moving down Powder River to its mouth, they came to the Yellowstone. The Indian trail still led eastward, but Crook needed to replenish his provisions before renewing the chase. [19] As Terry put it, "It was thought to be imprudent to enter upon the country lying between the Powder and Missouri Rivers without the full amount of subsistence which our pack mules could carry." [20]

Unfortunately for Crook, supplies were not immediately available, and he had to postpone his pursuit until provisions arrived from the mouth of Rosebud Creek. Most urgently he needed grain for his horses. The delay was caused by the difficulties experienced by the supply steamer in navigating the Yellowstone's low water. Crook waited impatiently, somehow deluding himself that the Indians would remain together and make his task easier. He consulted none of his officers or guides when pondering the Indians' intentions, a slight that dismayed his staff and angered his scouts. Cody resigned from the expedition in

disgust and started east after the supplies arrived.[21] At Fort
Buford on his way down the Missouri, Cody denounced
the entire operation to a newsman:

He said plainly that the soldiers did not want or intend to fight;
that he had worn himself out finding Indians; and, when he did
discover their whereabouts, there was no one ready to "go for
them." To use his own language, it was evident to him that no
one connected with the army had lost any Indians, and consequently they were not going to hunt any. He said he had
pointed out fresh trails, and they had been pooh-poohed as old;
and, when he reported bodies of the enemy, no troops could be
got ready until all hope of successful pursuit had faded away.
This, and much more to the same effect, fell from the lips of the
noted scout, who seemed untiring and outspoken in his denun-
ciation of the entire business.[22]

Cody's sentiments were shared by others on the campaign—the field operations had degenerated into a cumbersome management problem with a questionable future.
Lieutenant King surmised that as long as it remained under Terry's leadership the command "would never catch,
kill or scare 40 Indians. . . . The caution of Headquarters
surpasses everything."[23] To make matters worse, the Utes
and Shoshonis, convinced that the joint column would
never catch the Sioux, also left Crook at this time. These
scouts apparently perceived hardships awaiting them,
since they were by and large unfamiliar with the inhospita-
ble Dakota terrain. Perhaps more important, it was annuity
time at Washakie's agency.[24] Many of the civilian volunteers
left Crook too, along with several officers and enlisted men
who claimed illness, real or imagined, since leaving Goose
Creek. They were taken down the Yellowstone on steam-
boats. "A dinner on the boat, a sight of the comfortable
sleeping quarters there, and then a look at the wet camp on
the hills, and the thought of bacon and hardtack, was more
than their courage could stand," wrote a correspondent.[25]

To compensate for the loss of his Shoshini scouts, Crook acquired several Arikaras to accompany him, lent by Terry. After five days of virtual inaction Crook longed to be on the trail again. Doubtless tempers became sensitive as Crook grew impatient to be on his own, away from the restrictive presence of Terry.[26]

The supply boat arrived on August 23. Crook outfitted his force as meagerly as before, with each man rationed for fifteen days. He prohibited all extra baggage beyond blankets, overcoats, and rubber blankets. A dismal rain fell on the soldiers on the night before departure. Campfires hissed and steamed in the darkness, and the men sought shelter any way they could. Strong winds whipped the cottonwoods under which General Crook stood wrapped in a blue overcoat, finally causing him to seek cover elsewhere.[27] A newspaperman described officers without proper mess gear, using pieces of hardtack for plates and with but one fork for six people. "The solitary fork was from choice, the continuous rain was not, and under it the enthusiasm for simplicity had slightly washed out."[28] The next morning, soaked and miserable, the armies of Terry and Crook started back up Powder River to locate the Indian trails they had abandoned a week before. Word from army guard units on the Yellowstone, however, soon persuaded Terry that some of the hostiles would attempt a crossing and drive for Canada.[29] With this fear uppermost, Terry separated from Crook on August 26. Soon after, on September 5, he dismantled his force, returned to Fort Abraham Lincoln, Dakota, and, in accordance with Sheridan's new policy, proceeded to disarm Indians at the Sioux agencies. Colonel Miles and the Fifth Infantry remained to patrol the Yellowstone through the winter of 1876–77.[30]

On August 26, freed at last to his own designs, Crook headed east toward the Little Missouri. If the Indians lay somewhere between him and the Yellowstone, he might drive them in Terry's direction, or vice versa. Having received assurances of the availability of supplies at Fort Lincoln, on the Missouri River, Crook sent instructions for his wagon train, still in Wyoming, to move to Custer City, in the southern Black Hills of Dakota, where he expected eventually to meet it.[31]

Chapter 3
Hunger and Mud

GENERAL CROOK'S DEPARTURE from the Powder River in late August, 1876, marked the beginning of one of the most grueling marches in American military history. The weather, already bad, turned even colder as unseasonal rainstorms punished the soldiers almost constantly over the next three weeks. On Sunday, August 27, the column passed into the treeless, rolling land around O'Fallon Creek, a stream distinguished, noted one observer, for having "the most adhesive mud on the American continent."[1] The next day the men paralleled the trail made by the Terry-Custer contingent three months before. The day was unusually clear until dusk, when lightning ignited the grass in front of the troops. A heavy rain-and-hailstorm extinguished the blaze but frightened the horses and thoroughly drenched the men. The resulting mire proved particularly vexatious; as Finerty noted, "The horses sank in the mud to their kneejoints, and the soldiers' shoes were pulled off in trying to drag their feet through the sticky slime."[2] Yet this storm was light compared to the one that struck the command three nights later. Lacking any shelter whatever, the men turned their backs to "hailstones two-thirds as large as a hen's egg." Horses stampeded by the tumult galloped off into the darkness; some jumped into a stream and drowned.[3]

To conserve rations and to prevent scurvy among his soldiers, Crook proposed that they eat cactus and Indian turnips, which abounded in the area. Some of the men tried frying prickly pear, but the experiment generally failed and in a number of instances induced chronic dysentery. With the increased dampness and cold more sickness occurred, particularly diarrhea, neuralgia, and rheumatism. Two officers came down with malarial fever and had to be transported by horse-drawn travois. One man suffered a rattlesnake bite.[4]

All during this time the civilian and Arikara scouts searched ahead for Indians. On August 31 the trail began to divide, and the next day, along Beaver Creek near Sentinel Buttes, Frank Grouard discovered the first hard evidence of the tribes' scattering. The troops proceeded cautiously, and over the next few days they occasionally glimpsed small parties of warriors. But the tribesmen maintained a safe distance, precluding all pursuit, and by the time Crook's army reached the Little Missouri River, in present-day North Dakota, the main trail had disappeared altogether. Only vestiges of tracks remained, paths running south and east in the general direction of the agencies. More warriors were seen with each passing day, and once Grouard found four cast-off ponies and brought them into camp. Late one night some emboldened warriors fired on Crook's pickets, but with no success.[5]

On September 4 the column forded the Little Missouri at the point where Terry and Custer had camped in May. The corn on which their horses had fed had taken root, and Crook's soldiers now found stalks growing ten to twelve feet high. The men availed themselves of this unforeseen though meager supplement to their dwindling rations. Later that day the scouts fought a long-range duel with the Indians, wounding one warrior and killing a pony.[6]

Sporadic fighting again occurred the next afternoon, when the scouts stumbled upon what proved to be the Indians' rear guard. It started when a small number of warriors appeared some distance ahead of the scouts. The latter, with Major Stanton (the "Fighting Paymaster") in command, dashed off in pursuit, chasing the Indians for nearly five miles, until suddenly they were joined by a larger party that turned and charged the scouts, who precipitately retreated. One scout, Baptiste ("Big Bat") Pourier, whose horse was exhausted, dismounted and prepared for the worst. Two other scouts, Jack Russell and Baptiste ("Little Bat") Garnier, joined him for the defense, while the others continued their retreat. Somehow the little band managed to dissuade the Indians, and after exchanging a dozen or so shots, the warriors withdrew from the scene. Twenty minutes later Stanton rode back and proposed that they go after the hostiles again. Pourier, infuriated at having been abandoned by his colleagues, told the major: "If you want to go for them, go on. We are not going." Stanton later reported the incident to Crook, who spoke to Pourier about it. Pourier explained that he had been deserted, and the general expressed sympathy with Big Bat's caustic reaction.[7] The skirmish represented the first substantive action that any part of the expedition had experienced since leaving Goose Creek, and Crook was irritated because he had not been promptly informed about the apparent proximity of a hostile village. Although he pressed his command forward, the warriors withdrew under cover of a dense fog.[8]

On September 5, Crook camped at the head of Heart River. That evening he wrote Sheridan of the scattering of the hostiles: "With the exception of a few lodges that had stolen off toward the Agencies," he observed, "there was no change in the size or arrangement of the village until it disintegrated. All indications show that the hostile Indians were much straitened for food and that they are now traveling in small bands, scouring the country for small game."[9]

In the same dispatch Crook indicated his intention to march for the Black Hills, 180 miles due south, a greater distance than he would have had to travel had he chosen to

Baptiste ("Big Bat") Pourier, a well-respected and extremely competent guide on the northern plains. Courtesy of the Nebraska State Historical Society, Lincoln, Nebraska.

go to Fort Lincoln to provision his troops. He believed it imperative to safeguard the mining communities from incursions by warriors returning from the Big Horn country. Once he was in the Black Hills, the general would operate

out of a base to be established at Custer City, and he therefore asked Sheridan to have delivered to that point twenty
days' ration of fresh vegetables for his army and 200,000
pounds of grain for his animals.[10]

Crook's decision to strike out for the Black Hills pro-
voked considerable debate among the ranks, who were in-
creasingly fatigued from the constant whipping winds and
cold, enervating rainstorms. With but two days' rations
left, many men sick, and the horses growing weaker, the
plan drew loud condemnation.[11] Most of the soldiers had
hoped that the general would seek supplies at Fort Lincoln, while the others had expected him to opt for Terry's
depot, at the mouth of Glendive Creek on the Yellowstone;
either place could be reached in only four or five days'
march.[12] Also, many of the officers and men worried openly
about the advisability of trekking across the unknown country on the south. "There is a feeling of uncertainty . . . settling down upon us," wrote Lieutenant Bourke in his diary:

We have great confidence in Crook, but cannot shake off a pre-
sentiment of dread as to the possible consequences of our bold
plunge, without rations, across an utterly unknown zone of such
great width as that lying between us and the Black Hills. Frank
Gruard [sic] says he knows nothing of the country this side of the
Little Missouri river.[13]

The Black Hills lay at least seven days away, but Crook ob-
jected to going to Fort Lincoln or the Yellowstone. He expressed genuine concern for the safety of the Black Hills
communities, and his attitude was well founded; since July
roaming bands of hostiles had threatened settlements in
the southern Black Hills.[14] Furthermore, the freshest Indian trails led south, and Crook still hoped to strike the
Sioux and inject some belated morale into his troops. If he
deserted his objective now, the summer's campaign would
appear a wasted exercise.[15] Finally, and perhaps significantly, Crook probably wanted to avoid whatever influence

Scout Baptiste ("Little Bat") Garnier, seated at right beside Chief Red Cloud of the Oglala Sioux. Standing, left to right, are Chief Knife and Jack Red Cloud. Courtesy of the Nebraska State Historical Society.

Terry might exert over his maneuvers should he show up at Fort Lincoln.

His decision made, on the evening of September 5, General Crook ordered his command on half rations—enough food, if conserved, to last the soldiers four days.[16] Protected from the rain by a blanket, Captain Andrew S. Burt composed a letter for a Cincinnati newspaper in which he soundly endorsed Crook's leadership. Oblivious to the irony of his statement, he wrote: "To have met and worsted Sitting Bull, to have terribly punished him and his butchers would be a satisfaction to any man calling himself an American." He continued:

Under no other general of our army would we have accomplished as much. I suppose, in fact know, there are opinions strongly to the contrary; that possibly the majority of the papers of the country have [expressed] adverse opinions to this, but my belief is [that] this is an injustice to us and to him, which will be acknowledged.[17]

After nightfall, amid a steady rain, the Arikara scouts left camp for Fort Lincoln, bearing Crook's message for Sheridan in Chicago.[18]

In the morning the soldiers steered south from Heart River beneath a quickly fading sun. So deep was the stream that a bridge had to be built of boxes of ammunition from the packtrain.[19] More and more rain fell until the surrounding ravines were flooded. The land, wrote Finerty, became "wet as a sponge, but without elasticity." His boots, alternately soaked and dried, could not be removed; several cavalrymen went two weeks before taking their boots off. Likewise, infantrymen suffered from poorly constructed shoes that permitted the screws holding top and bottom together to wear through the soles and gouge the feet.[20] "All the unlucky combinations of a lifetime have culminated on this campaign," mourned one officer.[21]

Lack of adequate food now began to aggravate the physical discomfort of the troops. The fifteen days' rations carried from the Yellowstone had nearly been exhausted. There was little coffee left; sugar and salt washed from the packsaddles, and hardtack became soaked.[22] Even tobacco had given out; no one, recalled Lieutenant King, "can begin to imagine what it meant to the soldier to be without it on such a campaign."[23] Occasionally the men shot and cooked a few prairie dogs and rabbits, supplementing the fare with wild onions, wild plums, and bullberries. Many prairie-dog towns lay in the line of Crook's march, and the little animals stood curious and squeaking atop their mounds as the soldiers trudged by. A huge Newfoundland dog called Jack, which accompanied the troops, chased the creatures but never caught one. Two of Crook's civilians shot a hawk and a prairie dog and tried to cook them in an army cup filled with water, but the fire they built of wet grass was so smoky that it blackened the water and "made a sorry mess of the meat," which they had to discard.[24]

Lieutenant Bourke described the ensuing commotion whenever a jackrabbit entered camp: "The soldiers armed with lariats, nose bags and halters advance from all sides and keep up pursuit until the poor little jackrabbit is fairly run to death. There is enough shouting, yelling and screeching to account for the slaughter of a thousand buffaloes."[25] After the tobacco was gone, the remaining luxuries consisted of but two cans of jelly, a few pounds of beans, some tea, and a few canned goods. All these Commissary Officer Lieutenant John W. Bubb, Fourth Infantry, distributed among the medical personnel for future use. Only the scouts and civilian packers had conserved their rations since leaving the Yellowstone, and occasionally members of Crook's staff shared these resources without the general's knowledge. The dearth of food particularly angered the soldiers, and Crook came in for strong censure for having previously ordered short marches and for staying unnecessarily long in bivouac.[26] "Our hope," wrote Bourke, "is to overtake the main body of the hostiles in a day or two and get a fight which shall partially compensate us for our privations and sufferings."[27]

In worse shape than the soldiers were the pack mules and cavalry mounts. With the grass either burned by the hostiles or uncured and inedible, the animals slowly starved.[28] As Charles King remembered:

Earlier in the summer the long column of infantry, burdened only with their rifles and ammunition, would set forth on each day's march an hour ahead of the cavalry, to be overhauled and passed before noon. Once across the mud flats of the Little Missouri, all this was reversed. We of the mounted service would set forth as soon as the men had finished morning coffee and scraps of bacon, but in an hour most of the command would be afoot, dragging their dejected steeds, and long before noon, gaunt and wiry, those blessed doughboys would be striding alongside and then ahead, casually asking could they give us a tow.[29]

The languishing condition of the animals, together with the growing hunger of the troops, created a certain inevitability. As early as September 4, Bourke had noted that "the conviction is forcing itself upon our minds that we cannot avoid the alturnative [sic] of starvation or killing and eating our mules and horses."[30] Crook's determination to reach the Black Hills heightened that inevitability even more.

Until this necessity arose, however, the packers and cavalry troopers remained committed to the welfare of their beasts. They talked to the animals and, emulating Crook's chief packer, Tom Moore, rubbed bacon fat on their sores and prepared saddle blankets and pads so as not to chafe their broken skin.[31] All was for naught, however. More and more of the weak animals had to be abandoned. Each day additional mounts collapsed in the mud, some rising to stumble or be dragged after the command. Crook finally ordered all abandoned mounts shot. Captain Anson Mills of Company M, Third Cavalry, recalled:

I, with my squadron, was rear guard & Crook ordered me to shoot all played-out horses & we shot 70 that day that we found turned loose as we came along. About ⅓ of the cavalry men were afoot, and some of the officers were afoot, especially those who had taken no extra horses along. I had two good horses. John F. Finerty was afoot and he did not like it because I would not permit him to ride my extra horse.[32]

The demoralizing atmosphere created by the frequent gunfire soon forced Crook to cancel his decree. Many of the creatures dropped by the wayside and died from exhaustion.[33]

The rain squalls continued, and deluge followed deluge. "It is now more than a month since we had a change of clothing," reported Bourke. "We have been reduced to one suit worn in all kinds of weather, tropical heat and bitter cold, fervid sun and soaking rain."[34] The dreaded word came down from Crook on September 5: abandoned horses were to be shot each day for food at the rate of three per cavalry battalion. Officers and men alike found the directive practically cannibalistic. Many believed that the animals deserved better, and it appears that mules provided the staple until September 7, when the first horses were killed, butchered, cooked, and eaten.[35] Thereafter troopers could be seen carrying "quarters of beef" through camp in the evenings,[36] while "the carcasses without the hams and other choice parts could be seen here and there along the trail in the rear of the command."[37]

The unwanted feast took place grimly and silently. Stated one participant sarcastically: "Most of the command were compelled from sheer starvation to take advantage of this privilege."[38] Recalled another on his partaking of the diet: "There was not fat enough on a dozen horses to season the gruel for a sick grasshopper." Furthermore, he added, they were "eaten with no seasoning whatever."[39] The horse-and-mule diet lasted for several days, although some men put off eating the meat for as long as they could. In honor of

A posed picture taken by Photographer Stanley J. Morrow after the Crook expedition arrived in the Black Hills. The soldier is about to shoot a worn-out, exhausted cavalry horse, which was to be cooked and eaten, a reenactment of what actually happened during the campaign. Courtesy of the Custer Battlefield National Monument.

Some of Crook's soldiers butchering a dead horse, a scene re-
enacted for the benefit of photographer Stanley J. Morrow. Courtesy of the W. H. Over Museum, Vermillion, South Dakota.

the occasion, and with all the aplomb of an incipient pa-
leontologist, Lieutenant Colonel Carr dubbed the bivouac where he reluctantly took his first bite of horse meat
"Camp Hippophos, Dakota."[40]

On Wednesday, September 6, the army labored thirty
miles through a merciless drizzle. The men crossed both
branches of the Cannonball River, in what is now Slope
County, North Dakota, and then entered an uneven terrain,
barren of all growth save cactus and broken by swollen

streams and occasional alkali-impregnated water holes.
With no fuel except what grass could be made to burn, the
men went without coffee day and night. Riding ahead in a
mist, the scouts again drew scattered shots from Indians
still moving in advance of the army. Occasionally the men
in the column glimpsed distant warriors flashing mirror sig-
nals to their tribesmen. But the cavalry horses were too
weak by now to give chase.[41]

That evening Dr. McGillycuddy entered in his diary:
"Moved camp 30 m. South. Camp on Head of Bear 6 m.
S.W. from Rainy Butte. Rations ¼ minus the bacon.
No wood to cook the bacon we did not have. Clay water.
150 m. north from Deadwood City. 14 horses abandoned."[42]
For the same date Bourke entered the following, similar
notation:

At dark 30 @ 35 miles reached a couple of large pools of akaline
water and went into camp. There was not a single stick of wood,
not one as big as my finger. We resorted to the device of boiling
coffee by fires fed with such dried grass as could be culled in the
crevices and cracks of the soil. Little trenches were dug with our
knives, a cup filled with water and bearing the allowance of
ground coffee placed over it, [and] the fire started. . . . The
water was so alkaline neither horses nor men could touch it, and
in boiling it threw up to the surface a scum of saline and sedimen-
tary matter which made the coffee look decidedly repulsive.

He closed abruptly: "Command wet, cross, hungry, and
disgusted."[43]

The downpour had abated by the morning of September
7, when the command resumed the march. That day the
men crossed several Indian trails leading south, but Crook
could not pursue.[44] Men were now collapsing with the
horses as rain fell again in the afternoon. One participant
remembered the soldiers "stringing out fully twenty miles
on the road, weary, sore, half sick and dejected."[45] So dis-
consolate became the soldiers, wrote Lieutenant Walter S.
Schuyler, that "I saw men who were very plucky sit down

and cry like children because they could not hold out."[46]
The sick rode in litters pulled by exhausted animals, while
debilitated infantrymen mounted the backs of empty pack
mules. During the day dispatches from Terry reached
Crook, telling of supplies available at the Yellowstone, but
Crook by now was too close to the Black Hills to countermarch. The general decided to mount a detachment on the
strongest horses to press urgently on with the pack mules
and get provisions for his famished troops from the northernmost Black Hills mining towns.[47]

After consultation with Colonel Merritt, Crook assigned
leadership of the escort to Captain Anson Mills, who was
commanding a squadron of the Third Cavalry. That evening, as the command went into bivouac, Mills learned
that he was to select fifteen men, those with the least-worn
mounts, from each of the ten companies of his regiment
and leave that very night. Lieutenant John W. Bubb, expedition commissary, would command the pack train and at-
tend to the purchase of supplies.[48] His orders from Crook
read:

The Brigadier General Commanding directs you to proceed
without delay to Deadwood City and such other points in the
Black Hills as may be necessary, and purchase such supplies as
may be needed for the use of this command, paying for the same
at the lowest market rates. You are also authorized to purchase (2)
two ounces of Quinine, for the use of the sick.[49]

In Bubb's charge for the trip were Chief Packer Moore and
fifteen assistants, who would load and manage sixty-one
mules.

The escort under Mills consisted of 150 specially selected
Third Cavalrymen, a force divided into two battalions of 75
men each. One was commanded by First Lieutenant Em-
met Crawford, the other by First Lieutenant Adolphus H.
Von Luettwitz. Assisting them were Second Lieutenants
George F. Chase and Frederick Schwatka. The bearded

Mills, forty-two and a seasoned Indian campaigner, held brevets for "gallant and meritorious service" during the Civil War. A native of Indiana, Mills had entered West Point Military Academy in 1855 but stayed less than two years. He had gone to Texas, where he surveyed the site for El Paso, hence his occasional designation as the father of that city. A younger brother, Emmett Mills, had been killed by Apache Indians in New Mexico in 1861. In that year Anson had reentered the service at the outbreak of the Civil War and continued as an officer through the battles of Murfreesboro, Chickamauga, and Nashville, and during the Atlanta campaign. Mills was known among his colleagues as a competent, if sometimes ostentatious and abrupt, officer who could be counted on to do his soldierly duty. At Powder River in March and at the Rosebud in June, Mills had commanded a cavalry battalion, and Crook had recognized him as a dedicated, able leader. In later years Mills would devise, patent, and earn a fortune on the famous Mills Woven Cartridge Belt, adopted for army use in the United States and abroad.[50]

Two of Mills's subordinates would also gain notice in later years. Twenty-six-year-old Lieutenant Schwatka, an 1871 West Point graduate, would become an eminent explorer, commanding the famous Sir John Franklin Arctic search expedition of 1878 and 1879 and later heading scientific expeditions to Alaska and Mexico. Lieutenant Emmet Crawford, a veteran of the Civil War and many Indian campaigns, would eventually be killed by Mexican irregulars in a provocative border incident of the Geronimo campaign a decade after Crook's march against the Sioux.

Of the remaining officers, the Prussian-born Adolphus Von Luettwitz was a graduate of the Artillery and Engineer School in Berlin and had participated in various European campaigns as a member of the Prussian and Austrian armies. He had seen extensive service in the American Civil War, had been cashiered from the army and then reinstated, and was known among his fellows for his lively temperament. Lieutenant Bubb was a Civil War veteran too, and had been assigned to the Fourth Infantry since 1869. Like Schwatka, Lieutenant Chase was an 1871 graduate of West Point. He had served with the Third Cavalry for little more than four years.[51] Others who accompanied Mills's party included scouts Frank Grouard and Jack Crawford and two newsmen, Robert Strahorn of the *Rocky Mountain News* (Denver) and Reuben Davenport of the *New-York Herald*. Charles R. Stephens was assigned as medical officer.[52]

Mills later maintained that Crook gave him specific instructions to attack and hold any manageable hostile village he might encounter on his march.[53] Lieutenant Bubb, however, recalled overhearing Crook's orders and reported that the general had told Mills to avoid a fight should he encounter a large village and instead "cut around" it and go on to the Black Hills to get the supplies. Clearly that was Mills's prime mission. Crook also told Mills that he expected to remain in bivouac all the next day, September 8, to rest his command.[54] Mills therefore could not expect Crook's immediate support should he actively engage any Indians. Mills determined to travel light and permitted his men only fifty rounds each for their carbines. Despite the strictures imposed by Crook's instructions, the prospects for some type of action rejuvenated Mills's soldiers, for that day the scouts had found a broad Indian trail headed south. His arrangements completed, Captain Mills started out with his party at seven in the evening, just as the rest of Crook's command labored into camp near Grand River after another grueling trek of over thirty miles.[55] "Clothing and blankets wringing wet," wrote one disgruntled soul.[56]

Despite lingering hopes of recouping some of the summer's losses by actually striking the hostile tribes, catching them was obviously not now uppermost in Crook's mind, as Mills's departure into the murky darkness aptly illustrated.

It was a desperate move. Crook had overestimated—and overextended—both the resolve of his men and his resources. As Bourke had earlier mentioned, there was still an outside hope that a captured village might provide sustenance, but for now the Indians became of secondary importance to the survival of Crook's command.

Ironically, hostile tribesmen in large numbers were now nearer at hand and perhaps more accessible than at any other time since early summer. Many of the smaller camps had loosely congregated, intending to go to the Red Cloud and Spotted Tail agencies in northwestern Nebraska, south of the Black Hills. Not all were bound for the agencies, however. Many of Sitting Bull's and Gall's Hunkpapas appear to have been in the area too, though by that time some had begun concentrating in the region of the lower Yellowstone, preparatory to moving north into Canada. Other Hunkpapas, with Sans Arcs and Minneconjous, gathered on the east around Antelope Buttes, seeking trade with the Arikaras and fattening their ponies.[57]

An assemblage of tribesmen in present-day Harding County, South Dakota, along the South Fork of Grand River, contained Oglalas, Brulés, and some Cheyennes, among them Crazy Horse and his followers who were bound for Bear Butte.[58] Well supplied with dried buffalo meat and wild fruit, these groups drifted southward in small camp units that maintained constant association with each other. One mixed camp of Minneconjous, Oglalas, Brulés, and Cheyennes numbered thirty-seven lodges, probably around 260 people, and contained several minor Sioux leaders.[59] One of these was the Minneconjou American Horse, also known as Iron Plume, Iron Shield, and Black Shield. Other leaders with the camp were Roman Nose, an Oglala (not to be confused with the Cheyenne leader of that name killed at Beecher Island, Colorado Territory, in 1868); and Red Horse, Dog Necklace, and Iron Thunder, all Minneconjous.[60]

Doubtless historical reference to the camp as "American Horse's village" derives only from his known, active presence there at the time of the fighting. Before the action at Slim Buttes, American Horse was not well known to whites. He was reportedly the son of the old Oglala chief Smoke, who had met Francis Parkman in 1846. This Indian is often confused with an Oglala leader of the same name who in 1876 was just coming into his own as an effective orator and negotiator in behalf of his tribe.[61]

By September 8 the small village, en route to the Spotted Tail Agency, was encamped along both sides of the tributary of the Moreau River called by the Sioux Mashtincha Putin, literally Hairy Lip but translated Rabbit Lip.[62] (Today designated Gap Creek, the stream has its source immediately east of Reva Gap through the Slim Buttes range, just one and a half miles west of the village site. Gap Creek constitutes a branch of nearby Rabbit Creek, itself a tributary of the Moreau.) Several smaller streams converged from the north and east near the center of the camp.

The village lay compactly in a broad depression, protected on the north by a high, grassy ridge and across the stream on the south by a sharply rising, foliaged embankment that rolled gently away to the buttes beyond. The tipis were clustered about the various ravines and rivulets that crisscrossed the bottom. The wooded area, offering spring water and good grazing land, afforded the tribesmen potentially good hunting while at the same time concealing them from the army scouts.[63] Broadly encircling the village on the north, south, and west were the spires of Slim Buttes, the low-lying range of chalk-colored limestone and clay summits capped with pine trees that stretched twenty miles southward and two to six miles east to west. The name Slim Buttes was also derived from the Sioux, whose descriptive term for the feature means "thin butte" in the horizontal (north–south) rather than the perpendicular sense.[64] At Slim Buttes the people of American Horse, Red

Horse, and Roman Nose rested, unaware of the closing proximity of Captain Mills and his soldiers.

After leaving Crook's column, Mills's party rode for five hours through the rainy darkness. Once they stopped at a small pond full of water. Here Grouard struck a match, and the glow disclosed a muddy turf torn up with pony tracks, indications, said the scout, of a large camp nearby. At midnight, after making eighteen miles, the men paused, picketed their mounts, and tried to fall asleep on the soggy ground. At 4:00 A.M. on September 8 they were off again without eating. Three hours later they were skirting the eastern slopes of Slim Buttes, where they stopped and breakfasted on wild plums. Although the rain had let up, a heavy, dense fog now settled uneasily over the landscape, limiting visibility. At eight Mills resumed the march and kept moving until noon, when the men enjoyed coffee while the horses grazed.[65] The troopers pushed on, with Lieutenant Crawford's detachment in the lead.

That afternoon the fog lifted, and Grouard, riding ahead, spotted some Indian hunters whose ponies were piled high with game. Around 3:00 P.M. the scout discovered a small herd of ponies grazing four miles ahead and close by the Buttes, certain evidence of a village nearby.[66] Apprised of the discovery, Mills continued to advance. About two miles from the herd he ordered his command into a coulee, and he and Grouard briefly surveyed the countryside. Then Mills returned to the command and consulted his officers, most of whom, at the outset, favored attacking the camp. He ordered his troops to countermarch half a mile northeast of the supposed village area, until they reached a draw about 150 feet deep with a stream running through it. There they dismounted.[67] Mills proceeded with his reconnaissance, hoping to determine the size of the camp and plan a course of action against it.[68]

Mills's intelligence mission was not productive, owing partly to Grouard, who, Mills discovered, was afraid of ap-

Captain Anson Mills, who was responsible for attacking the Indian village. In after years he made a fortune designing and manufacturing his webbed field equipment for the army, but he was denied the Medal of Honor he sought for his performance at Slim Buttes. Courtesy of the National Archives.

First Lieutenant Emmet Crawford. Extremely capable, he survived the attack on American Horse's village but was killed by Mexican irregulars during the Geronimo campaign in 1886. Courtesy of the National Archives.

proaching the village too close. He later commented that Grouard "knew the ways of the Indians, and was, undoubtedly the best guide we could have found for such knowledge as that, but in many ways he was not to be relied upon. I always regarded him as a coward and a big liar."[69] Grouard searched ahead and reported to Mills that the village was too large for his force to assault, a warning Mills chose to ignore because, as he put it later, "I had not much confidence in Grouard as a fighting man."[70] Together the two men approached near enough to see part of the herd and a few of the lodges, but they could not advance closer because they feared arousing dogs in the camp. Grouard later claimed to have entered the camp and stolen two Indian ponies.[71] Mills recollected the episode:

I . . . told Grouard to go ahead & find the exact location of the village. Grouard went off and remained a long time, and when he returned I noticed that he had a new horse. He had been riding an Indian pony that was thin and nearly used up. He had gone up to the herd, unsaddled, caught a fresh horse . . . & saddled it. He was acting so cowardly and hesitatingly, that I at once suspected he was getting himself in shape to get away should we get into a hot fight. . . . I was afraid the herd would smell us & stampede into the village, and [I] scolded Grouard for having gone among them, but he was a good deal like an Indian and the ponies seemed not to take fright at him, as he was riding an Indian pony.[72]

In all, Mills learned little about either the size of the village or its occupants. Grouard obtained little pertinent information, and his actions seem to have jeopardized Mills's command while it lay so close to the Indian camp.[73]

The Indians themselves seem to have been oblivious to the approach of soldiers. They knew that Crook's army was in the vicinity but evidently knew nothing of the proximity of Mills's detachment. Late that afternoon, as the cavalrymen waited in hiding, they suddenly spied a solitary warrior slowly riding toward them along a high ridge. Fearing

Frank Grouard, born a Polynesian but raised by Indians; who served as Crook's chief scout in 1876. He seems to have been every bit as ambivalent in personality and capability as his contemporaries depicted him to be. Courtesy of the Nebraska State Historical Society.

detection, the officers ordered sharpshooters to pick him off if he came nearer. The Indian, however, apparently seeing nothing through the growing darkness, turned his pony about and headed back toward the village.[74] Mills's soldiers breathed a sigh of relief.

The night went slowly, "one of the ugliest I ever passed,"

remembered Mills, whose men huddled under cottonwoods in the cold while rain fell nearly a foot deep in
places.[75] Years later Mills recalled the details of that long,
suspenseful night:

> I gave orders to the officers not to permit any of the men to leave
> the ravine but we were wet and cold and I consented to permit
> them to build fires, which they did. After the fires had been built
> I saw a peculiar thing. The clouds were low and as they passed
> over us the light of the fires would illuminate them much as a
> search light does the sky on a dark night. I was afraid this would
> discover us to the Indians, but the weather was bad and they
> were not on guard.[76]

The hungry soldiers ate what little bacon and hardtack they
had, and the packers devoured a soupy concoction of flour
and grease. Once in the night the pack mules tried to run
off but were restrained by their picket ropes. The men and
horses, "crowded like bees" in the draw, rested uncomfort-
ably if at all.[77] Perhaps the soldiers had thoughts of the Custer catastrophe, for the reporter Davenport remembered
that "a dull apprehension of disaster reigned."[78]

Such harrowing thoughts were indeed present when
Mills and his subordinate officers met to contemplate their
situation. The captain advocated a surprise attack at day-
break. Although ignorant of the size of the village and its
strength, Mills was, as he later asserted, "willing to take
my chances in view of General Crook's positive orders" to
attack any village encountered.[79] The facts of the matter
seem to suggest, however, that Crook had mentioned this
possibility only in the event that Mills came across a very
small encampment and had ordered that otherwise a fight
of any kind should be avoided and the Indians bypassed for
the more urgent task of obtaining the needed supplies in
the Black Hills. In the course of the debate Lieutenant
Bubb, who was second in rank to Mills, appealed to the
captain to send Crook word of the encampment. Mills re-

fused.[80] In any event, Mills at this juncture had very little if any solid information with which to determine the size of the hostile village. Under these circumstances his juniors were inclined against what appeared to be a blind assault, especially in light of the similar conditions that had preceded Custer's fall. Yet Mills argued forcibly, philosophically, and persuasively that much of success in warfare rested upon chance and advantage. Advantage lay with the concept of the strike at dawn; indeed, one army maxim held that any large body of Indians would scatter before a well-implemented cavalry charge. Moreover, urged Mills, failure to deliver a vigorous blow now could bring discovery and pursuit by the tribesmen after daylight, and the condition of the army horses forecast trouble for the troops in that eventuality.[81] Faced with so unpromising an alternative, the officers subscribed to their captain's reasoning, albeit somewhat reluctantly.

The matter settled, Mills proceeded to carry out the classic military tactic of the Indian Wars period, an ancient design resurrected in response to the unconventional nature of warfare with the Plains Indians—the attack at dawn. This tactic, though never formally stated, was in part an extension of the annihilation philosophy fostered by Generals Sherman, Sheridan, and Ulysses S. Grant during the Civil War. On the plains the maneuver of surprise and destruction, augmented philosophically by the "total-war" concept, worked best against elusive tribesmen who seldom stood and fought. The most successful assaults occurred at daybreak, with three or more columns of soldiers striking a sleeping camp simultaneously.[82] Against such disconcerting thrusts defense was futile, and warriors rushed from their lodges only to be cut down in the charge. Tragically, large numbers of women and children often died in the confusion of the dawn strike. Once sacked, the village with its supplies was burned, and the ponies were killed. Tribesmen subjected to the tactic of surprise at dawn experienced psychological shock and abjectly surrendered. Humanistically speaking, the tactic was immoral, but for an army charged with subjugating the Sioux and other dissident Plains tribes, it was justified for the simple reason that it worked.[83]

Thus it was this tactic that Captain Mills planned to employ against the sleeping village. The specifics decided upon were as follows:

The plan of attack was to approach the head of the village in the morning with three parallel columns, the outer two being dismounted; the right, numbering fifty-seven men, under Lieutenant Crawford, Third Cavalry, and the left, numbering fifty-three, under Lieutenant A. H. Von Luettwitz, Third Cavalry, to diverge respectively to the right and left, with extended intervals as skirmishers, and surround the village. The center column of twenty-five men, mounted, as soon as the daylight was sufficient to see the front sights on the carbines, or sooner, if the Indians discovered our presence, was to charge with pistols, and stampede the herds of Indian ponies. The herd being well away, a sufficient number could dismount at the further end of the village, and close the gaps between the columns of Lieutenants Crawford and Von Luettwitz.[84]

If the attack succeeded, the camp would be sacked, its warriors killed or captured, and its provisions distributed among Crook's needy soldiers or destroyed. The engagement would be over in one clean sweep, and the first real army victory of the Sioux campaign would be won. The Battle of Slim Buttes was about to begin, and Mills was confident of its outcome, though he knew neither the size of the camp nor the number of warriors it contained. That battle would involve twists and turns that Captain Mills could not foresee.

Chapter 4
First Glory?

BETWEEN 2:00 AND 3:00 A.M., Captain Mills formed his command and moved out in the direction of the enemy encampment. Fearful that the braying mules might betray him, Mills left them and 125 horses behind in the control of Lieutenant Bubb, the packers, and twenty-five soldiers. Bubb was instructed to advance with the livestock as soon as he heard firing from the village.[1] It took about an hour of "floundering through mud and water" before the cavalrymen, most of them dismounted, reached the north ridge above the Sioux camp. Lieutenant Schwatka led the twenty-five mounted soldiers who, according to Mills's plan, would actually charge through the clustered lodges. Lieutenant Crawford was ordered to post his fifty-seven troopers in skirmish order on the long ridge north and slightly east of the camp, while Lieutenant Von Luettwitz began moving his fifty-three soldiers farther east and south of the tipis, to the ridge across the stream. Both of these commands prepared to open fire on the lodges and close in afoot once Schwatka's men had driven through, routed the ponies, and cleared the village area.[2] "The object," reported a newsman, "was to surround the enemy, stampede and capture their stock, and kill as many of the warriors as possible."[3]

Schwatka arranged his mounted unit several hundred yards away, on a sloping ridge formed by two draws that finally converged close to the north edge of the village.

Near the village end of this ridge, as well as in the bottom-
land, grazed about 400 ponies, scarcely visible in the misty
morning darkness.[4] The camp slept soundly, smoke from
the tipi fires hanging low beneath the clouds and obscuring
the lodges. The soldiers were still making final disposi-
tions, waiting for enough daylight to be able to aim effectively.[5] But before Von Luettwitz's men could surround the
southeast flank of the camp, the soldiers startled the pony
herd and the animals began neighing excitedly. The herd
began running directly for the village, tearing through and
waking its occupants.[6] At this, Mills quickly sent Schwatka
in on the charge:

I had told Schwatka to be ready to charge on the village the instant the pony herd would stampede, for I knew the minute they
smelled us they would start and run into the village. . . . When
the herd stampeded Schwatka followed them right into the village, riding through it and firing with pistols into the lodges. He
chased the herd through it, knocking down and trampling over
some of the lodges.[7]

Soon Mills ordered the dismounted cavalry troopers to
open fire on the lodges from their positions north and west
of the camp. As Schwatka swept beyond the village and
captured much of the Indians' livestock, the soldiers of
Crawford and Von Luettwitz advanced, firing, to within
fifty yards of the camp, their bullets sounding "like hailstones" as they struck the wet buckskin and canvas tipis.[8]
But the warriors responded vigorously, slashing exits in the
tipis on the sides opposite the troops. The fleeing warriors
managed to unleash one or two volleys at the soldiers, and
Lieutenant Von Luettwitz fell almost immediately, a bullet
shattering his right kneecap as he stood on a knoll next
to Mills. Instantly Jack Crawford rushed over, tearing off
the neckerchief he wore and fashioning a tourniquet about
Von Luettwitz's wounded leg to check the flow of blood.
Sergeant John A. Kirkwood carried Von Luettwitz behind

Brave and adventurous Second Lieutenant Frederick Schwatka, who led the cavalry charge through the Indian village at Slim Buttes at dawn on September 9, 1876. Schwatka gained fame commanding various polar explorations, but died a young man in 1892. From *Harper's Weekly*, 1878.

the ridge to safety, while the frightened, angry warriors covered the flight of their women and children from the camp. Private Orlando H. Duren of Company E, Third Cavalry, received a wound in the thigh during this initial fighting.[9] Lieutenant Schwatka described the assault from his perspective:

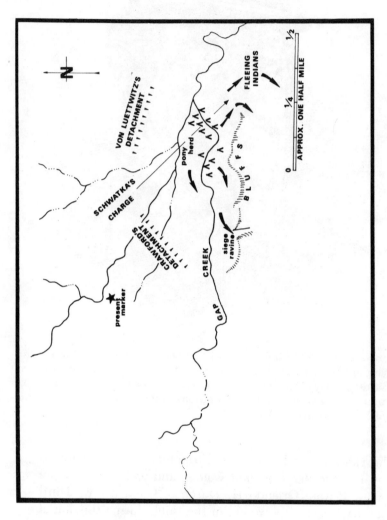

The Battle of Slim Buttes, September 9, 1876: Mills's attack at dawn.

The mounted party, pistols in hand, yelling and firing into tepees, rushed through the little town and soon depopulated it of
ponies, and gave the human population such a morning reveille
as they did not have to awaken them at every daylight. The dismounted men followed up the mounted charge rapidly with a
deadly fusillade into the village. The night having been very
rainy, the Indians had securely fastened the openings in their
lodges, and it was with evident impediment that they made their
exits. Many were seen to fall, and in the approaching daylight it
was often hard to tell whether the burdens carried were children
or the slain and wounded.[10]

Most of the Indians fled south and west, splashing
through the swollen creek and scrambling into the heavy
underbrush south of the stream bed and up the adjacent
bluffs. The warriors followed suit, taking advantage of
Mills's failure to secure an effective cordon southwest of
the tipis. Several of the tribesmen sought refuge in a deep
ravine that bordered the high bank on the south.[11] These
Indians fired sporadically at the soldiers, as did a few warriors who had posted themselves among the rocks and
ridges south of the Gap Creek draw. For some time, wrote
Mills, "we did not crowd the village."[12]

As the tribesmen gradually withdrew, however, Mills's
troopers, unable to shoot accurately in the misty light,
rushed the camp. The lodges and their equipage appeared
to be largely intact, for the Indians had scarcely had
enough time to escape with their weapons. From one tipi,
later believed to be that of American Horse, Private William J. McClinton of Company C retrieved a cavalry guidon stripped in June from Custer's command.[13] After half
an hour of brisk firing, daylight slowly revealed to Mills the
object of his assault, and he found the camp lodges full of
meat, berries, and various Indian accouterments. South
and west of the village Mills saw warriors riding back and
forth through gaps in the buttes, and he grew worried lest
another village should be nearby, a possibility acknowl-

edged by the apprehensive Grouard. By this time the soldiers had used up much of their allotted ammunition, and
Mills sent back word to bring forward the horses and pack
animals in Bubb's care.[14] Bubb was already close by, having
begun to advance, as ordered, upon hearing the shooting
from Mills's attack. When Bubb arrived, Mills ordered him
to send two messengers back over the trail "and tell Crook
that I had a village & was trying to hold it and needed assistance." The lieutenant chose two men, a packer and a soldier, provided them with good mounts, and ordered them
to ride fast "even if they had to kill the horses." The two
rode away bareback, ready to run on foot if necessary. Later
Bubb sent a man to the high, rocky butte a mile north of
the camp under instructions to watch for Crook and signal
his approach to Mills's command.[15]

Presently the firing stopped. Mills kept up his guard,
however, for many Indians could be seen on the bluffs on
the southwest. Crawford's soldiers were sent in groups of
five through the village to check tipis and collect stores.
"There were no Indians," remembered Sergeant Kirkwood, "so we started to collect the dried meat, of which
there was an abundance, all packed in raw hide sacks."[16]
Meantime the firing resumed as warriors returned to the
area after having conducted their families to safety. Although Mills was firmly in control of the camp, he soon
found his skirmishers under attack by Sioux and Cheyenne
marksmen bent on attacking his wounded. In response,
Lieutenants Bubb and Crawford mounted small detachments and succeeded in keeping the warriors at bay. According to Bubb:

Crawford & I established a chain of attack posts in a circle around
the whole command, Lt. Crawford taking the Rocky [sic] sides,
dislodging about all the Indians who were annoying us from that
direction. I took the eastern side of the circle. This is the manner
in which we held the Indians at some distance until arrival of
Genl [sic] Crook & command.[17]

The Indians made several abortive rushes, hoping to recapture some of their ponies. Strahorn of the *Chicago Tribune* reported that "a number of the most gallant dashes were made at them by Lieut. Crawford at the head of 10 or 12 cavalry. His efficient conduct was marked by rare judgment, coolness, and bravery."[18]

Nevertheless, under the annoyance of the long-range firing, Mills found it impossible to search the camp thoroughly and devoted most of his time to securing and defending it until Crook's arrival. Most of the soldiers took up positions atop the ridges north and east of the village, and, at Lieutenant Bubb's urging, Mills had his men dig entrenchments on the ridge across Gap Creek facing the wooded ravine in which the small group of Sioux men, women, and children had taken refuge.[19] An officer recounted the following incident regarding these Indians:

Some dried meat could be seen hanging from poles in the village, and [Correspondent] Robert Strahorn . . . and several packers volunteered to accompany the scout [Jack Crawford] and if possible secure the meat. A pack mule was taken along. Just as they entered the village the mule was killed by a shot from the Indians in hiding near by, and the men quickly jumped into the bed of a dry waterway which ran near. No one could locate the spot from which the shots had come. Jack cried out to Schwatka who was up on the hill asking him if he could with his glasses see any smoke from the discharged weapons, and on receiving a negative reply said he would endeavor to ascertain the location of the hiding Indians by drawing from them another shot. He sprung out of the creek bed, ran forty or fifty feet and reaturned [sic] and halted on the creek bank. A bullet came whizzing by him, and pointing to where it struck the ground and then in a directly opposite direction he cried to Shwatka [sic] that the shot came from where he indicated, and levelling his glass the lieutenant saw a curl of smoke rising from a ravine near by, bordered with scrub trees and underbrush. A detachment of soldiers was despatched to a point from which they could fire and prevented the Indians from firing on the party in the village until they could load themselves with the meat and escape back to the command on the hill.[20]

These Indians felt no urgent need to surrender, for, as they defiantly yelled over to the soldiers, more Sioux camps were at hand and their warriors would soon come to free them.[21] This news must have made Mills and his officers apprehensive about whether Crook could arrive in time, since the general had said he would remain bivouacked through September 8 at the place Mills had left him, far to the north. Boldly proclaiming their defiance, the Indians sheltered in the ravine and concealed by thick foliage took a great many potshots at the troopers. Some of the men tried to approach from the west side near enough to shoot into the gully. One, Private John Wenzel of Company A, ill-advisedly approached the ravine from the front. He died instantly as a Sioux bullet slammed into his forehead. To this first army fatality of Slim Buttes Sergeant Kirkwood applied the cliché: "He never knew what hit him."[22] Kirkwood himself, along with Company M's blacksmith, Albert Glawinsky, and Sergeant Edward Glass of Company E, tried to dislodge the Indians. Lamented Kirkwood: "It was no go. They got me in the side, only a flesh wound, but close. A little more, and the backbone would have been broken. Sergeant Glass had his arm shattered. The bullet went in at the wrist, and came out at the elbow."[23] After this episode Mills sent yet another messenger—the third—to Crook.[24] Short of expendable men and ammunition, the captain prudently decided against further efforts to expel the Indians from the ravine. They too would await General Crook's personal attention.

General Crook's column was not far behind. Unknown to Mills and his subordinates, the general had decided against remaining in camp on the North Fork of Grand River. Probably the increasing abundance of Indian signs, coupled with growing anxieties about Mills's command, influenced his change of plan.[25] Instead of resting his troops as he had intended, he drove them inexorably onward, with

"viscous mud sticking to the feet and making advance almost impossible."[26]

On the night Mills left the command, several weary
stragglers, including a surgeon, had reached Crook's camp
long after dark, and the soldiers had subsisted on quarter-
strength coffee boiled over rude fires fueled by rosebushes
and twisted grass.[27] On September 8 the army took up the
march directly on Mills's trail. "For breakfast—water and
tightened belts," commented Lieutenant Schuyler.[28] More
horses were abandoned during the day; toward evening
others were shot for food. Rain fell incessantly, a cold wind
blew fiercely, and the hours passed with the same dreary
monotony of the preceding days. The scouts managed to
kill several pronghorn antelope, and this success, along
with the discovery of some firewood and wild plums, raised
the men's spirits somewhat that evening. One soldier
jotted in his notebook: "Horse flesh was issued and although no salt was issued to the Command the Men appeared to eat the Meat with great relish. The broiling and
roasting was kept up all night and the morrow's Rations was
consumed at once before the Men was satisfied."[29] These
rations were but a quarter of the normal daily allowance.[30]
Some idea of the agonizing straits now faced by Crook's
army is found in this excerpt from Bourke's diary:

By this time the rations at Hd Qrs. had run down to barely
enough bacon to fry the horse-steaks needed for another meal.
Of salt and sugar we had none whatever and of coffee so little,
that our cook had great reason to felicitate himself upon the tur-
bid water found in the streams we camped by as it partially concealed the weakness of the beverage served up to us. Hard
bread, too, had come to an end . . . [but for] six little biscuits and
Deadwood still five (5) days away![31]

That evening, after covering the twenty-four miles to the
South Fork of the Grand,[32] Crook's officers congregated

around the campfires and tried to celebrate the general's forty-eighth birthday, but it proved more a simple assembly than a party. Observed Bourke: "Nothing to eat, nothing to drink, no chance to dry clothes, and nothing for which to be thankful except that we had found wood."[33]

With the troops now extremely low on rations and tired of the horsemeat menu, criticism of Crook's leadership again arose, and even Colonel Merritt expressed anger at the conduct of the campaign. One soldier was overhead to say outright that Crook should be hanged.[34] With tempers thus strained the command retired for the night. Some of the men, taking advantage of the first campfires in several days, lost precious sleep trying to dry their clothing and blankets.[35] Nearby in the murk loomed the northern spires of Slim Buttes.

At dawn on September 9 the expedition marched away in a cold downpour. The soldiers left camp in columns of twos, some walking, others mounted on their half-dead horses. About five miles out they encountered Mills's first two messengers, who hurried forward with the first news of Mills's assault on the hostile camp, reckoned at seventeen miles ahead.[36] An officer described the event:

Two horsemen appeared amidst the mist and rain, to the head of the column galloping, and as they shot past it is all we could hear, Mills had a fight. . . . Soon General Crook comes from the rear, and we learn that Mills had charged on a village.[37]

Soon another messenger came in and told Crook that Indian reinforcements would probably arrive soon and that Mills needed relief at once. Mills's casualties, he reported, stood at one soldier killed and five or six wounded, and medical aid was urgently needed.[38] Instantly Crook directed Merritt forward with all the Second, Third, and Fifth Cavalrymen who still possessed mounts capable of advancing.[39] The relief contingent, led by Crook, numbered about 250 men and 17 officers, plus surgeons Clements and McGillycuddy and some pack mules loaded with medical stores. The troopers moved off in a slow trot at 7:00 A.M., while the infantry and remaining cavalry soldiers pressed on vigorously behind, excited by the prospects of battle.[40] That morning there appears to have been much pointed argument among the officers over the propriety of Mills's attack on a hostile village of uncertain size, a controversy intensified by Custer's defeat under like circumstances. The question was especially provocative since Mills had opened the engagement with but a small supply of ammunition.[41] According to most contemporary witnesses, Crook could scarcely contain his anger at Mills. "Mills had discovered the village the evening previous," wrote his adjutant, "but had not sent back word as he should have done, to General Crook. Hence, when he attacked at day-break, he found himself unable to surround the village . . . and just barely strong enough to maintain himself . . . until the arrival of General Crook, for whom he was now only too glad to send."[42] Bourke continued: "Mills' conduct in this feature cannot be commended, but he is entitled to praise for the plucky manner in which he attacked and carried in the darkness of the morning, a village of unknown strength and resources."[43]

The criticism of Mills's action seems to have been universal, and was reflected in the columns of the press representatives. Crook's friend Strahorn wrote: "Crook was very much disappointed because Mills didn't report his discovery last night, and there was plenty of time to have got the entire command there and so effectually surrounded the village that nothing would have escaped; but the General is also pleased, all things considered."[44] Reuben Davenport of the *New York Herald*, whose relationship with Crook's command was at best antagonistic, reported that the development "chagrined" Crook even more because it seemed a repetition of the September 5 encounter, about which he had been informed too late to chastise the Sioux effectively.

Davenport offered a stinging rebuke to the precipitate action of Captain Mills:

All the circumstances lead to the inevitable conclusion that had Col. Miles [sic] reported the discovery to headquarters, instead of attempting to steal a march on the camp himself, the whole column could easily have reached and effectually surrounded the entire village before daylight. More than this, the weather, which has rendered the march so hard, was all that could have been desired for the purpose of getting up to our enemy either by night or day. A dense fog enshrouded the country far and wide, and instead of this large village of over 250 to 300 hostile savages getting off with whole skins, they could easily have been swooped down upon and annihilated.[45]

In fairness to Mills it should be noted that, despite an impulsive nature that undoubtedly contributed to this action, he believed at the time that Crook was still bivouacked on the North Fork of Grand River. In that belief, Mills must have felt that even if he had made contact with Crook it was doubtful that the command could have marched the roughly thirty-five miles to the camp and have been in position to strike at dawn.

Led by General Crook, Merritt's weakened cavalry took four-and-a-half hours to reach Mills's battleground, arriving at 11:30 that morning after a difficult trek across the soggy terrain. Fifteen more horses were abandoned en route. Bubb's sentinels sighted the troops two hours before they reached the village. "When we got their signal I tell you we breathed a sigh of relief," recalled the lieutenant. "Crook . . . saved us from total annihilation."[46] As the soldiers approached, a small party of hostiles appeared and swept down as if to capture some of the jaded animals stumbling after the column. Merritt's troopers fired at them, and the warriors withdrew beyond carbine range. The rest of Crook's command, nearly all afoot, struggled onto the village site throughout the afternoon. Cresting a ridge, the relief party beheld the two hundred or so ponies captured by Schwatka in the initial charge, corralled in the bottom near the tipis. Here and there lay a few dead ponies, the sole fatalities of Mills's initial attack. Mills's soldiers were scattered along a wide perimeter, securing the village, while most of their horses remained picketed along the hillsides.[47] At the campsite the men worked to dismantle the lodges and retrieve their contents. The area teemed with activity and looked, said one newsman, "like an anthill which had just been stirred up."[48]

Captain Mills greeted his relief and advised Colonel Carr of the armed warriors still ensconced in the ravine. Crook came up and asked to see the village, which was beyond the ridge. Mills warned him about the Sioux snipers, but the general walked away toward the tipis, recklessly endangering himself. Almost instantly he was shot at, but the bullet passed by harmlessly. Crook assumed charge, establishing his headquarters in the creek bottom near the lodges, some distance east of the warrior-occupied ravine. A short distance on the west Carr headquartered the Fifth Cavalry, while directly north of Carr, on the ridge from which Schwatka had charged the camp, Colonel Merritt posted his headquarters. Other officers established their respective unit stations on the west and north, behind the ridge across from the Indian sharpshooters' hiding place. In the meantime Crook surveyed conditions and distributed the troops at selected defense points. Earlier Mills had removed one of the larger tipis to a secluded spot beside a northern tributary of Gap Creek, and there his wounded soldiers were taken. At this improvised field hospital Dr. Clements examined the casualties and, with his assistants, deliberated about whether to amputate Lieutenant Von Luettwitz's right leg. The army horses, most of them too worn out to require picketing, found shelter at the rear, along muddy watercourses close to company lines.[49]

Crook's command now proceeded to collect everything of value from the lodges. They pulled down the remaining tipis and separated the stores to be saved from the greater number to be destroyed. The camp, much larger than Mills had anticipated, held thirty-seven lodges as well as four tipi frames without covers.[50] Though Mills's assault had seemingly failed to kill a single inhabitant of the camp, confiscation of the contents provided ample compensation for Crook's starving soldiers. To them the village bequeathed a wealth of goods. An inventory of the supplies found there noted sacks of flour, corn, and fruit; and packages of beans, salt, pepper, and tobacco. Utilitarian goods included guns, saddles, harnesses, clothing, blankets marked "U.S.I.D.," canvas, boxes of percussion caps and ammunition, metal cooking utensils and dishes, several bolts of calico, some knives, forks, and spoons, and 2,000 unbound buffalo, antelope, elk, and deer skins. Of special consequence to the troops was some freshly killed game and over five thousand pounds of dried meat, "a God-send," remarked one hungry soldier.[51] Crook allowed Mills's soldiers first choice of souvenirs. The other troops then took what they wanted of what remained.[52] The village, wrote Captain Burt, "is filled with soldiers wandering about, muddy, tattered, lean and gaunt, rather sleepily lounging around looking over plunder, scattering over prized paint and porcupine quills, nosing about robes and para fliches [sic]."[53]

During the search of the village some of the men discovered a three- or four-year-old girl. "She commenced crying and screaming," remembered Grouard, "and she ran everybody out of the lodge. When she began to cry and yell, the soldiers supposed there were more Indians in the lodge and they got out in double-quick time."[54] She was taken to Captain Mills, who at first decided to adopt her but subsequently dropped the idea after contemplating the prospect of facing Mrs. Mills with such a *fait accompli.*[55] Most unsettling to the soldiers was the discovery of evidence directly linking these Indians to the Little Big Horn. Besides the swallow-tailed guidon, Crook's men found at

least one gauntlet marked with the name of Captain Myles
Koegh of Company I, Seventh Cavalry, who died with Custer; several McClellan army saddles; three Seventh Cavalry horses; several orderly books; an officer's blouse; some
letters written to and by Seventh Cavalry personnel; and a
large amount of cash.[56] But what really incensed the soldiers was the discovery of a certificate issued to one of the
Indians the previous winter by the agent at Spotted Tail:

> Whitestone [Whetstone] Agency, D.T., Feb., 1876.
> *To any United States Indian Agent*:
> This is to certify that Charging Crow, an Indian belonging to
> Santee's band, is a true man to terms of treaty, and uses all his
> influence with his people to do right. I cheerfully recommend
> him to favorable considerations of all.
> Yours, respectfully,
> E. A. Howard, United States Indian Agent[57]

Another pass, authorized by a reputed "illicit trader and
brother-in-law of Spotted Tail," the Brulé leader, was also
found among the effects in the village:

> Spotted Tail Agency, Jan. 14, 1876.
> The bearer of this, Stabber, belong [*sic*] to this agency, will travel
> North to visit his people. He will return to this agency within 90
> days, without disturbing any white man. If he needs any little
> thing you will not lose by giving it to him. This is true.
> F. C. Boucher[58]

While the Little Big Horn relics left little doubt among
the soldiers that they had struck some of the hostiles who
had destroyed Custer, there in fact existed implications
that not all the warriors in this village had taken part in the
event. Years afterward certain Indians asserted that the
Little Big Horn articles Crook found at Slim Buttes had
been brought among American Horse's followers by visiting Oglalas[59] and that they had been victimized by association. Yet there remains abundant evidence that at least

some of the warriors who were with American Horse on
September 9 had taken part in the Custer fight. The Minneconjou Red Horse admitted his presence at both encounters, as did other Sioux.[60] The possibility that the village at
Slim Buttes contained some Indians who were not veterans
of the Little Big Horn most probably was not seriously en-
tertained by the troops of Mills and Crook now that they
were at last poised on the threshold of success.

The search of the village by Crook's men was complicated by the Sioux snipers still hidden in the densely covered ravine, and Crook soon turned his efforts to dislodging them. The winding gully ran some two hundred yards
back into a hillside. In places it was nearly twenty feet
deep, and its narrowness kept the soldiers from firing accurately into it unless they stood along its edges. To judge by
the changes in the ravine over the past century, the bottom
must have been between six and fifteen feet wide. Trees,
thornbushes, and other tangled shrubbery covered the entire length, obstructing any view of the interior. The Indians already had killed one soldier, and were threatening all
who approached. Barricaded behind dirt breastworks and
in wall pockets that children had originally dug, the occupants, anticipating succor from other villages in the area,
geared for a stout defense. Uncertain about how many warriors were concealed there, Carr had placed sentinels at a
safe distance around the ravine. Some of the scouts and
packers joined in an informal attempt to roust the Indians,
but they met with unexpected firepower and fell back in
surprise.[61]

Crook then ordered troops deployed near the stream
bed below the mouth of the gorge, and they crawled forward on their bellies, firing at random into the hidden re-
cesses of the ravine, without evident harm to the warriors.
Before long a multitude of soldiers had gathered near the
cavelike mouth of the ditch, somewhat protected from gunfire by a sharp embankment. Officers and men joined in

sending a fusillade into its black depths, and suddenly they received a veritable volley in response that sent them reeling and stumbling away.[62] Crook and his entourage took up positions on the west side of the ravine. Opposite them on the east side and close to the edge of the embankment lay three of Crook's scouts, Charles (Jonathan) White, Baptiste "Big Bat" Pourier, and Baptiste "Little Bat" Garnier. White, known by the sobriquet "Buffalo Chips," was described by Bourke as "a good-natured liar who played . . . 'Sancho Panza' to Buffalo Bill's Don Quixote."[63] He lay between Pourier and Garnier and, despite their remonstrances, was determined to get off a shot into the ditch. Just as he raised himself to take aim, a Sioux bullet ripped into his chest, knocking him off the embankment and into the lower part of the gulch. White was heard to utter, "Oh, God!" as he fell dead below.[64] Private Edward Kennedy of Company C, Fifth Cavalry, had the calf of his leg blown away in a barrage, and Private John M. Stevenson, Company I, Second Cavalry, received a severe ankle wound.[65] In the meantime, Pourier managed to shoot one of the Indians and then descended into the ditch, scalped him, and miraculously escaped unharmed—all in a matter of seconds.[66]

The deaths and injuries of their comrades inflamed the soldiers, who were already distraught from their two-week ordeal. On Crook's orders First Lieutenant William Philo Clark led a group of twenty volunteers forward to oust the Indians, who, however, sent forth such overwhelming volleys that the troops scampered for safety. Some of the men crept forward with flaming sticks, which they tossed into the ditch without apparent effect.[67] By now so many idlers had gathered in the vicinity of the ditch that they complicated the efforts of Clark's men. "It was a wonder to me," recalled Bourke, "that the shots of the beleaguered did not kill them by the half-dozen."[68]

The sharpshooters again approached the edge, braving the hidden danger to deliver a point-blank discharge from their weapons. This volley evoked cries from women and children, the first indication that Crook gained that there were noncombatants in the ditch.[69] Immediately he ordered all firing to cease, but the dozens of soldiers, overcome with anger, surged forward. With difficulty Clark managed to control his sharpshooters; other officers rushed in and began literally to beat back their men. In the melee soldiers pressing forward jostled Captain Samuel Munson of the Ninth Infantry and Adjutant Bourke, both of whom tumbled into the lower part of the gorge, landing near a number of women and children who were "covered with dirt and blood and screaming in a perfect agony of terror."[70] Protected from the warriors by the ravine's natural bend, the two men quickly scrambled up the side and rejoined the troops.[71]

Firing now ceased entirely while the general urged Bat Pourier and the hesitant Grouard forward to negotiate the Indians' surrender. The scouts moved warily toward the gully, and Grouard called out to the occupants, telling them their lives would be spared if they came out. Finally Pourier entered the ravine, where he met "a woman in great distress of mind, wet and numb and shivering," who pleaded with him for her life. Suddenly an armed warrior appeared. Bat jerked the Indian's revolver from him and tossed it out of the ditch, seized the woman, and took her, the warrior, and another woman and a ten-year-old girl out of the gully. He turned the captives over to an infantry company. When the other women and children saw that the captives were unharmed, they also emerged. One carried a dead child with her. Another carried an infant whose foot had been shot off; the child soon died.[72] In all nearly twenty women and children had sought refuge in the ravine.[73] As they climbed out, they crowded around Crook, wrote Lieutenant King,

each eager to grasp the General's hand, and then to insert therein the tiny fist of the papoose hanging in stolid wonderment on her back. One of the squaws, a young and really handsome woman, is shot through the hand, but she holds it unconcernedly before her, letting the blood drip on the ground while she listens to the interpreter's explanation of the General's assurance of safety.[74]

The warrior occupants refused to leave, however. They fired again, forcing the soldiers to dive for cover. Exasperated by the increasing casualties in his ranks, Crook now directed some of his infantry and dismounted cavalry to form up across the creek facing the opening of the gorge. On signal the troops opened a steady, withering fire on the ravine that reportedly sent an estimated three thousand bullets among the warriors.[75]

After a while the shooting stopped as Crook once more offered immunity to the holdouts. An hour passed quietly. Again Grouard and Pourier moved forward and succeeded in opening a dialogue in the Lakota tongue.[76] Then one of the captive women volunteered to talk with the intransigents; she succeeded in coaxing out one young man, who received Crook's personal assurances of safety for all who surrendered.[77] Again Pourier entered the ditch. More minutes passed. Then a tall Sioux appeared, teetering, at the mouth of the draw, supported by Bat and another warrior. The Indian had sustained a serious wound in his abdomen, and his bowels protruded into his clutched hands as he was helped out to meet Crook. The general took his proffered rifle and instructed Grouard to ask his name; the Indian replied in Lakota, "American Horse." Pourier helped him to two surgeons. One of them pulled the chief's hands away, and the intestines dropped out. "Tell him he will die before next morning," said the surgeon.[78]

American Horse's surrender occurred amid angry shouts of "No quarter!" from the watching soldiers. Then two more warriors emerged from the ravine, one of them wounded, making four men who had survived the onslaught. They had only twenty-four cartridges among them

An artistic (and erroneous) rendition of the surrender of American Horse at Slim Buttes. From George A. Forsyth, *The Story of the Soldier*, 1908.

when they came out.[79] Behind in the ravine lay three
women, one warrior, and one infant, all dead.[80] Crook ordered the bodies removed from the gorge. They had been
riddled with bullets. The women, reported one newsman
in the attitude of the day, "were quite pretty for Indians."[81]
Contemporary depictions of the scene, while ugly, nevertheless offer graphic illustrations of one saddening aspect
of the Indian wars period—the tragic deaths, usually acci-
dental, of noncombatants. Correspondent Joe Wasson described in grisly detail what he saw:

I was standing directly upon the place where the women had
come from, and heard the shouts of the men who were groping in
the hole of the bank underneath, that "there were more of
them." "Bring them out—drag them out!" yelled the crowd.
"There's a white man," was next heard in excited and half-
smothered tones from below. At this the mass of men above
seemed to go wild. "A white man!" was repeated from mouth to
mouth, and then rose a wild chorus of yells, oaths, and execra-
tions. "Drag him out!" "Cut him to pieces!" "We'll burn him
alive!" "Show him to us." There was no white man, however.
When the body was dragged into light, it proved to be that of a
squaw whitened by death. She was frightfully shot. A bullet had
torn her neck away, three had gone through her breast and shoulder, and two through each limb. Her body and clothing were one
mass of mud and coagulated blood. . . . Then followed the half-
naked body of the old Indian Big Bat had killed. It was very un-
ceremoniously hauled up by what hair remained and a leather
belt around the middle. The fatal shot had struck him under the
ear, and shattered the whole base of the skull. Another bullet,
evidently after death, had struck him under the left arm and
come out of the shoulder. The body had stiffened in death in the
posture of a man holding a gun, which was the way he was shot.
He was an old man, and his features wore a look of grim determination. After this came still another squaw, also shot in several
places. It seemed that the bodies of the women had been used by
the survivors as defences. They were all laid out, and the curi-
osity of the command . . . [was] satisfied by an inspection of an
hour or so.[82]

Ute John, the sole remaining scout of the Utes and Shoshonis—the others had left Crook back at the Yellowstone—proceeded to make a show of scalping the dead
females, an act emulated by some of the soldiers. "The ex-
hibition of human depravity was nauseating," commented a
witness, but apparently Crook's officers did little to curb
the demonstrations.[83] According to Bourke, at the start of
the fight the ravine had contained twenty-eight Sioux men,
women, and children. Miraculously, twenty-three survived
and were made prisoners.[84]

One of those who entered the gorge immediately after
the surrender was Captain Mills. The little girl who had
been discovered in the village lodge tagged along behind
him as he went to view the bodies. Suddenly the child ran
forward and fell upon one of the women's corpses, hugging
it tenderly. It was her mother, and the little girl wailed
pitifully. "The sight was enough to touch the heart of the
strongest man," recalled Mills.[85]

By late in the afternoon the scene at Slim Buttes was
peaceful. The noise of firearms had given way to the sounds
of women and children crying, dogs barking, and sergeants
shouting orders to troops tearing down the tipis in the village. At the field hospital the surgeons worked futilely on
American Horse. The chief refused morphine, preferring
to clench a stick between his teeth as Dr. Clements and Dr.
Valentine McGillycuddy tried to close the ghastly stomach
wound. Lieutenant Von Luettwitz fared better. He un-
derwent surgery that afternoon, when Dr. Clements removed his shattered leg above the knee. Despite fears for
his life Von Luettwitz rested comfortably and subsequently
recovered.[86]

From the captives Crook's officers learned of a large
Oglala camp of approximately three hundred lodges under
Crazy Horse, He Dog, and Kicking Bear in the area,
though none of the prisoners agreed on its precise location
and distance from Slim Buttes. The information nonethe-

less caused apprehension among the command, for ever since Crook's arrival a few Indians had been seen hovering in the distance. Some were even reflecting mirrors down on the troops from the high terrain on the south and west. The tired soldiers anticipated an assault once the refugees from Mills's attack could spread the alarm to other camps.[87]

That assault was not long in coming. By 4:15 P.M. the weary troops were settling into bivouac. The cavalry command was spread out for over half a mile along the ridge immediately northwest of the village and paralleling Gap Creek. The Fifth Cavalry was camped closest to Merritt's and Carr's headquarters; then came the Second and Third regiments. Horses of all the units were staked out among the adjacent swales and ridges on the north and south, while the mules and captured Indian ponies were corralled in the creek bottom near the village site. The ponies had been awarded to their Third Cavalry captors, and many of them had been put up for sale to those who needed replacements for their mounts. Just north of the village, around the improvised hospital, the infantry troops had set up their camp. In the creek bottom the remaining Sioux lodges and their contents lay in disarray. West of the ravine some soldiers and civilians assembled before the wrapped remains of Private Wenzel and Scout White, while an officer read the burial service. Along the bivouac line cavalrymen had stacked their arms and were preparing to dine on captured bison meat. Barking dogs and crying children accented the low conversation of the troops.[88]

Suddenly the sharp report of gunfire echoed across the bluffs on the west. The soldiers scrambled to their feet as the trumpeters blared forth with "To Arms!" They reclaimed their carbines and rifles and prepared for a defense. Gradually the shooting spread all around the arc formed by the southwestern buttes, as returning warriors attacked in an effort to recover their ponies and lost property and to free the hostages. The Indians were joined by members of the Oglala camp of Crazy Horse. Mounted on fleet animals, the warriors—variously estimated at six to eight hundred strong—advanced boldly to occupy advantageous positions on the high hills ringing the troops below. At stations three-quarters of a mile away along three low buttes many of the Indians congregated to direct concerted, long-range fire at the army.[89]

The first response of the troops was to protect their livestock, and Crook ordered a defensive line thrown around the ponies and mules, which had been picketed close to the village. Herd guards went quickly after the cavalry mounts and drove them into the protective circle. Each company then took up a position in front of its own horses, to shield them from the advancing warriors. Some of the Fifth Cavalry animals grew frightened in the tumult, fled beyond the guards, and stampeded south toward the Indians. Only the resolve of Corporal J. S. Clanton, who with scant help succeeded in turning the lead horse, prevented their capture. At the same time some warriors rode forward and managed to drive off a few of the abandoned cavalry mounts while under fire from the dismounted skirmishers.[90]

Just as the shooting erupted from the southwestern hills, Captain William H. Powell and Company G, Fourth Infantry, were preparing to burn the Indian village on Crook's order. They went on with their task as the fight intensified around them, and before long the huge piles of tipis, skins, saddles, and ammunition were ablaze.[91] The conflagration reportedly "shot out a perfume anything but grateful to the enemy and everybody else."[92]

General Crook deployed his men to answer the attack. He ordered Major Chambers's infantry battalion to take the high ground occupied by the warriors. Accordingly, two companies of the Fourth Regiment, one of the Ninth, and one of the Fourteenth, all under Captain Burt, moved out on a run from their bivouac location and raced through the burning village, through the stream, and up to the top of the cutbank that had partly sheltered the village. Three more infantry companies took up position behind the cutbank as supporting units and as guards against attack in that quarter.. The men of Company F, Fourteenth Infantry, led by Captain Thomas F. Tobey, posted themselves directly east of the siege ravine. Next to them was Company I, Fourteenth Infantry, commanded by Lieutenant Frank Taylor, while the left of the reserve line was composed of Company B, Fourteenth Infantry, under Captain James Kennington.[93]

Most of the battle occurred along the bluffs south and southwest of the village, but to secure the area north of the camp and keep the hostiles from approaching too close on the rear of the troops, Chambers dispatched two Ninth Infantry companies to the ridges above the area of the infantry bivouac. Similarly, the open eastern flank was held by Major Henry E. Noyes and a unit of mounted Second Cavalrymen, who would resist any assault by the warriors along that front.[94]

Noyes's men were the only ones mounted during the fray. The other cavalry units moved forward in skirmish order much as the infantrymen had done, determined to take the southwestern heights and drive the Indians before them. The first assault by the tribesmen had occurred directly in front of Major Julius Mason's Fifth Cavalry battalion, and as the line of men surged ahead, it was Mason's group that received the first casualties of the afternoon encounter. Sergeant Edmund Schreiber of Company K and Private August Dorn of Company D fell back wounded.[95] To Mason's left advanced the battalion of Major John J. Upham, Fifth Cavalry, while to his immediate right and on down the line were the units of the Second and Third regiments. Part of the Third, the regiment commanded by Lieutenant Colonel William B. Royall, stepped forward to take control of the hills to the west and northwest, but

Captain Andrew S. Burt, who led Company H, Ninth Infantry, during the afternoon encounter at Slim Buttes. Courtesy of the Custer Battlefield National Monument.

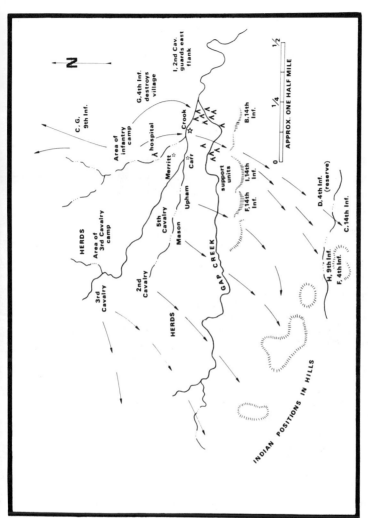

The Battle of Slim Buttes, September 9, 1876: the afternoon fight.

these troops saw little action. That was reserved for Carr's Fifth troopers, who moved forward in unaccustomed fashion on foot toward the foe who were on the low-rising southwestern buttes.

These soldiers and their infantry counterparts fanned out through the coulees and draws as they forged ahead, occasionally halting to discharge random shots at the distant warriors. For forty-five minutes they pressed on. Finally, on the left, three of Captain Burt's four infantry companies succeeded in driving the Indians from a high, rocky promontory. From that point the soldiers were able to level rifle volleys down an unobstructed draw to the west, routing the Indians who had been using it for cover. Company H, Ninth Infantry, under Lieutenants Charles M. Rockefeller and Edgar B. Robertson, assumed the extreme right of the skirmish line facing southwest from this knoll; Captain Daniel W. Burke commanded Company C, Fourteenth Infantry, on the left of the line; and Captain Gerhard L. Luhn commanded Company F, Fourth Infantry, in the center. Company D, Fourth Infantry, under Lieutenant Henry Seton, served as reserve and remained behind the skirmish line. Half the unit was soon called forward by Captain Burt and made part of the line. The Sioux and Cheyenne warriors maintained a distance of five to eight hundred yards and consistently fired their weapons so high that casualties among the infantry troops were few. Only one soldier was wounded in the advance. Likewise, however, the troops caused little harm to the Indians. An officer recalled that during the fight "one Indian was either Killed or wounded and one Pony Killed in our front."[96]

On the west, Major Upham's Fifth Cavalrymen gained the three hills that lay before them, and, aided by the infantry fire from the left, drove the Sioux away into the bluffs beyond. As the skirmishers pushed on, the Indians drew away, continuing their desultory shooting from afar.

The heavy, moist atmosphere imprisoned the smoke from the weapons, and it hung in a fog close about the troops as they ascended the foothills. Guns in all quarters rattled on after dusk fell. For a time some of the Indians held their ground, and at one point they charged the Third Cavalry contingent holding the northwest of the perimeter, but a well-aimed fusillade sent them racing away. Finally as night fell, the combined effort of the cavalry and infantry had its effect. The warriors gradually wavered and then withdrew completely into the Slim Buttes.[97]

The evening fight, while more an exercise than a decisive engagement, was nonetheless important for all of Crook's soldiers and made them forget, temporarily at least, the travail of past days. The Indians had gained the upper hand in position but had been forced to retreat. As reporter Strahorn described the encounter:

The field could not have been more advantageous for foes, as its speedily-occupied rock-covered bluffs commanded all approaches; yet the one hour's fight that followed was little more than a beautiful and impressive skirmish drill for our troops, and a very ungraceful flight from all positions by the savages.[98]

The picture was romantic: "As the shades of evening fell it was magnificent to see our skirmish line lighting up the mountain sides with their volleys."[99] Yet despite the victory in repelling the warriors, Colonel Carr grumbled that it "was a most wasteful expenditure of ammunition, [as] some companies fired as much as forty rounds per man."[100]

Considering all the shooting, losses on both sides were surprisingly light. Only five or six soldiers were wounded in the evening action. Sioux and Cheyenne casualties largely went unknown, for the warriors removed many of their dead from the field upon leaving. Lieutenant Colonel Carr wrote that "according to the best and most reliable accounts we killed and wounded as many as seven or eight

Indians."[101] Another, unofficial, account of the affair stated that "fourteen dead Indians were found on the battlefield, and four bodies were known to have been carried off."[102]

As the Indians retreated, the western clouds broke to reveal a brief crimson sunset. The soldiers returned to their camps. In the bottom a dozen bonfires had turned American Horse's village into a smoldering ruin from which dense, black smoke rose to blend with the storm clouds. Anticipating further assaults, Crook's officers posted strong pickets on the outlying hills and along the entrenchments earlier prepared by Mills and Bubb.[103] Several riderless Indian ponies were captured as darkness closed in. The animals—killed, butchered, and roasted—provided a welcome diversion from mule and horsemeat. Recalled Finerty:

Cavalry horse meat, played out, sore-backed . . . [and] fried without salt, [is] stringy, leathery, blankety, and nauseating. Cavalry horse, younger than preceding and not too emaciated, produces meat which resembles very bad beef; Indian pony, adult, has the flavor, and appearance of the flesh of elk; Indian pony, colt, tastes like antelope or young mountain sheep; mule meat, fat and rank, is a combination of all the foregoing, with pork thrown in.[104]

The pony meat drew converts almost immediately. "Fat, grass-fed Indian pony isn't half bad when men are hungry," remembered Lieutenant King.[105] One civilian packer even grew to like the diet: "I really thought that horse meat was good," recalled David T. Mears, "and wondered why we did not eat more horse at home."[106] The dried bison meat, which proved difficult to cook and to eat, was to be packed on mules for the march south.

The bivouac that night stood in marked contrast to earlier ones, as the men rejoiced in their newfound wealth of food and warmth. Wrote a newsman:

Night is here, and 1,000 camp-fires light a scene never to be forgotten. The soldiers last night, ragged, cold, weak, starved, and

Sioux Indians captured at Slim Buttes. These tribesmen, mostly women and children, remained with the soldiers when the other prisoners were released after the battle. The man standing at left is Charging Bear, who later became an army scout. Courtesy of the W. H. Over Museum.

well-nigh desperate, are feasting upon meat and fruits received from a savage enemy, or warmly clothed by the robes which last night wrapped the forms of renegades. Merry songs are sung, and everywhere goes up the cry, Crook is right after all.[107]

After supper Crook interrogated the Sioux prisoners, nearly all of whom were women and children. From them he learned that both Crazy Horse and Sitting Bull were in the vicinity of the Little Missouri and that the latter was headed north for Antelope Buttes to trade. Crook also learned that the Indians had indeed split up and that most of them were bound for the agencies. The general lectured his captives on the determination of the government to punish all those who remained hostile and then announced his intention to free them the next day.[108]

Through the night a drizzling rain fell on the soldiers. Despite their newly acquired robes they got little sleep because of the barking dogs and neighing ponies. A few men gathered to complete the burial of Private Wenzel, which had been interrupted by the late-afternoon encounter. Six soldiers who had left the column early that morning to hunt stumbled into the bivouac in the darkness. Knowing nothing of Crook's march to relieve Mills or of the subsequent action, these men reported having been attacked on the trail by a dozen warriors and held under fire for four hours before the Indians retired. Occasionally in the night the pickets fired into the mist at imagined or real foes. After midnight the skirmishing picked up, and at three o'clock Company G, Fourth Infantry, along with Companies B, F, and I, Fourteenth Infantry, assumed strong positions on the hills on the south and southwest, ready in case the warriors should return in force.[109] Throughout the night the medical personnel labored to save Private Kennedy, whose shattered leg required amputation. He did not survive the operation, dying near midnight in the surgeons' lodge. American Horse also died at about that time.[110]

Dr. (Major) Bennett A. Clements, medical director of the Big Horn and Yellowstone Expedition. Courtesy of the National Library of Medicine, Bethesda, Maryland.

The burial of Scout White and Private Kennedy took place early Sunday morning, September 10. The bodies were interred in one grave, along with Lieutenant Von Luettwitz's leg. Care was taken to conceal the location of the grave from the Sioux, a measure accomplished by burning fires on the mounds. Crook then ordered his cavalry brigade to march over them to obliterate their location, truly a fatuous exercise, carried out as it was in the presence of the prisoners and the distantly watching hostiles. The few remaining Indian dead were left on the ground to await disposition by their tribesmen.[111]

At dawn the warriors briefly resumed the fight, firing blindly at the troops through a fog that settled in the creek bottom. They withdrew when fired on by the infantry pickets. Meanwhile, Colonel Merritt directed Carr to destroy any remaining Indian property. Carr's cavalry troopers wrecked every article in sight, breaking guns, exploding ammunition, slitting and burning buffalo robes, and axing and crumpling tinware underfoot. The captured pony herd was to go south with Crook's column to provide both sustenance and fresh mounts. On Crook's authority Carr also released the prisoners. Some of the women and children voluntarily left the command, though quite a few decided to stay with Crook until they reached an agency. One of the male prisoners cast his lot with the general and later became an army scout.[112] There is no substantiating evidence for the charge made fifty-nine years later by a deserter from Crook's expedition that the captured warriors were shot to death by the troops before the command left the battlefield.[113] Soon the wounded who could not walk or ride were placed on stretchers rigged between two mules or on the more trustworthy mule-drawn travois, in preparation for the journey south. Von Luettwitz experienced such excruciating pain upon being moved that he tried to wrestle a pistol from one of the packers with which to kill himself.[114]

Acting Assistant Surgeon Valentine T. McGillycuddy, who was
placed in charge of Crook's wounded following the fighting at
Slim Buttes. He is shown standing beside a wickiup, or temporary shelter, during the march through the Black Hills. Courtesy
of the Custer Battlefield National Monument.

The Big Horn and Yellowstone Expedition pulled out of
the village site at about 9:00 A.M., its exit covered by the
infantry companies stationed on the southern hills. These
troops exchanged fire with distant warriors as the main column filed out of camp in twos and headed east along the

Two prizes retrieved from the Slim Buttes village, a buckskin lodge and a Seventh Cavalry guidon captured earlier by the Sioux from Custer's dead command. This photograph was taken after Crook's army had reached the Black Hills. Standing, left to right: Frank Grouard, Private William J. McClinton (who had captured the guidon), and Lieutenant Frederick Schwatka. Sitting, left to right: Lieutenant Colonel William B. Royall, Captain William H. Andrews, Captain Anson Mills, and Lieutenant Joseph Lawson. Courtesy of the Custer Battlefield National Monument.

Officers of the Third Cavalry in the Black Hills. Captain Anson Mills is seated at lower right, with hat on knee. Lieutenant Schwatka is seated behind and at the right of Mills. Courtesy of the National Archives.

plateaus fronting Slim Buttes. When the command had cleared the area, the infantry units began a smart withdrawal to rejoin their battalion, their movement in turn covered by two dismounted Fifth Cavalry companies under Captains Sumner and Montgomery of Mason's battalion. As the command moved away, the Indians advanced, and the firing picked up. At Merritt's direction Carr now ordered Major Mason's entire battalion to come in on the right to relieve the withdrawing infantry skirmishers, who now faced a direct attack from the warriors. The other battalion of the Fifth, under Major Upham, took up a position on the ridge directly south of the village site but soon had to retire under stiff fire from the Indians.[115]

Under these conditions the command pulled away, leaving the cavalry rear guard to occupy the Indians. Crook headed his army east a short way and then turned south along fairly level terrain. The infantry skirmishers soon overtook the column. Carr's cavalrymen sent their horses to join the command, while they withdrew from ridge to ridge in a lively contest with the Sioux. As the troops gained an eminence, the one just vacated by them filled with pursuing warriors. A few precisioned volleys interrupted one concerted attempt by the Indians to outflank the soldiers, though sporadic fighting continued over the next two miles. Two soldiers were wounded in the rearguard action, and at least five of the Indians were killed or injured. Guarded by skirmishers at his front, sides, and rear, General Crook pushed on toward the seemingly unreachable Black Hills, seventy miles away.[116] Late that day Captain Burt summed up: "Men are weary and hungry; one can see looking at the infantry line that the men stagger and are weak. . . . The excitement is over."[117]

Chapter 5
Campaign's End

GENERAL CROOK'S EXPEDITION covered fifteen miles on September 10 and went into bivouac early, at 2:00 P.M. The halt was made because of fears for the wounded, who experienced great discomfort on the unsteady, mule-drawn litters. They received close medical attention in the afternoon. Many of the soldiers passed the daylight hours fashioning crude leggings and moccasins from materials taken from the captured village. Colonel Carr had obtained a piece of canvas large enough to suffice as a two-man tent. This shelter he subsequently shared with Lieutenant King, who was faring poorly, the weather aggravating an old arrow wound he had received years earlier in Arizona.[1] During the afternoon Crook composed dispatches announcing to General Sheridan the first major army victory of the Sioux War. He reiterated his need for provisions and asked Sheridan to requisition for him "five hundred horses, preferably the half-breed horses raised on the Laramie plains or in the vicinity of Denver and already acclimated to this country."[2]

On the evening of the tenth, Crook sought volunteers to carry his dispatches forward. Grouard was directed to hurry "to Fort Laramie, Wyo, or the nearest point where you may find the telegraph line in working order and thence transmit dispatches to Lieutenant General Sheridan."[3] Grouard refused to go, however, even when Lieutenant Bubb volunteered to accompany him. Nobody went

that evening. In the morning General Crook ordered Mills
to ride ahead for provisions and to accompany Grouard at
least on the first leg of his journey with the dispatches.
Mills's command consisted of his own Company M, Third
Cavalry, and fifty men of the Fifth, a total of about seventy-
five. As before, Bubb as commissary officer was charged
with obtaining the supplies. Second Lieutenant George F.
Chase also went along, as did two reporters, Finerty and
Davenport. This time no mules were taken, and the soldiers were all mounted on some of the best of the captured
stock. In addition to acquiring food, Mills was to assess the
effects of the threat from the Indians on Deadwood and
other nearby mining communities.[4]

The weather continued bad that morning as Mills's
mounted unit pulled away. Much of the time the fog was so
thick that the soldiers had to be guided almost exclusively
by compass. Once during the day the command stumbled
upon an Indian trail fresh with steaming pony dung. The
discovery caused Mills no small alarm. He decided that it
would be best for the command to separate, thus ensuring
that at least part of it would reach the settlements on the
south. He and Bubb and about half the unit continued directly toward the Black Hills, while the other part, under
Lieutenant Chase, veered slightly east, ready to skirt the
Black Hills and reach Camp Robinson should Mills not suc-
ceed in getting provisions.[5]

Chase's command pushed southeast for hours, until well
after dark. Finally they reached a secluded spot with some
trees, and the lieutenant permitted his men to build a fire,
"a dangerous thing to do," as he recalled. "It was arranged
that if attacked by Indians each man had a place picked out
to get to in order to make a defense." Chase described an
incident at the campfire that revealed his men's hungry
state:

A suckling colt that had followed us all day and was about played out, staggered up to the fire, among the men, to warm himself. One of the officers proposed that we kill and eat him. I replied that I had been thinking of that myself, but had thought better of reserving him for an emergency; but the more we talked of the matter the more the idea struck us of having a meal right there & so it was decided to kill the colt. As soon as this intention was announced an eager soldier threw one arm around the colt's neck & with his other hand drew a knife and cut the colt's throat. In 15 minutes the men were eating the raw flesh of the colt, not even waiting to roast it.[6]

Soon after this incident Chase's troopers were startled by the sound of horses coming through the trees and bushes. They ran to their prearranged positions, ready to engage Indians. But the sounds proved to be those of a courier from Mills announcing his arrival, at about 7:00 P.M., at Crook City in the northern Black Hills. Chase and his men joined Mills there. Early on September 12 fifty head of cattle and ten double-teamed wagons loaded with goods started back on the trail to meet Crook.[7]

Meanwhile, Crook and his soldiers plodded south on Mills's trail, amid more pelting rain and aggravating mud. On the eleventh, after Mills had departed, the general ordered a contingent of Carr's cavalry to ride back to the Slim Buttes village site. Lieutenant Von Luettwitz in his agony had envisioned his leg being exhumed and mutilated by the Indians. Late in the day Major Mason's battalion returned to report that the bodies had indeed been removed from their graves and desecrated.[8] Crook's command that day steered a course diagonally across the lunar landscape of Slim Buttes, and then headed generally in a southwestern direction. Getting through the Buttes, however, was a particularly difficult enterprise. The escarpment became extremely rough, the misty pine-clad pinnacles giving way to sharply ragged cliffs that seemed to defy all topographical reason. Cavalrymen led their mounts stumbling down the

abrupt, rain-slickened faces, many horses and soldiers nar-
rowly escaping injury in the descent. Lieutenant King
recalled:

We arrived in amaze at a veritable jumping-off place, a sheer
precipice. . . . We had been winding along up, up, for over an
hour, following some old Indian trail that seemed to lead to the
moon, and all of a sudden had come apparently to the end of the
world. General Crook, his staff and escort, the dismounted men
and the infantry battalion away ahead had turned sharp to the
left, and could be faintly seen winding off into cloudland some
three hundred feet below. Directly in our front to the south, rolling eddying masses of fog were the only visible features. We were
standing on the brink of a vertical cliff, its base lost in clouds far
beneath.[9]

On the march that day more horses were abandoned and
shot. The wounded suffered. The travois carrying Von
Luettwitz overturned in a stream, eliciting a barrage of angry oaths from its occupant. Criticism of Crook's manage-
rial acumen returned full force with worsening weather
and marching conditions. The pack mules grew weak without forage, and several hundred pounds of ammunition had
to be unloaded and buried to ease their loads.[10] Occasionally the extreme despair of the men evoked humor that
somewhat relieved their psychological distress. Lieutenant
Schuyler recalled: "We saw a Cavalryman who, after getting his weak horse along as far as he could, unsaddled him,
shot him, cut out the tenderest steak he could find, built a
fire, and philosophically sat down to a hearty meal. This
finished, he shouldered his carbine and went on, re-
freshed."[11] It was a standing joke among the foot soldiers
that if the cavalry marched long enough the infantry would
eat all their horses.[12] Generally, however, laughter was rare
in the ranks of Crook's command as it coursed its way south
amid rain, mud, cold, and fatigue.

Late on the eleventh a rising mist disclosed the hazy out-
line of Bear Butte on the east and Inyan Kara Mountain

A two-mule litter bearing one of the casualties of the Slim Buttes battle. Courtesy of the Custer Battlefield National Monument.

west of the Black Hills, a consoling sight to Crook's men. Twenty-one miles of rough country were passed on that day, and the troops were strung out on the trail until late that evening. The column slowly wound its way south-

The camp of Crook's bedraggled army near the Belle Fourche River as photographed by Stanley J. Morrow. Courtesy of the Custer Battlefield National Monument.

southwest just east of Deer's Ears Buttes and made camp along the banks of the south fork of the Moreau, or Owl, River, a tributary of the Missouri.[13]

The worst was to come. September 12 proved to be the hardest day of the campaign, one that taxed the will of the men to go on. Sheets of rain fell on the command. The ground turned into a quagmire. Scores of horses were abandoned, and men killed the beasts and devoured the meat raw. Frantic with exhaustion, soldiers dragged themselves across the slimy, clinging turf and, wrote one of them, "cursed the God who made them."[14] Progress was further hindered by the sick and wounded, whose travois-bearing animals often bogged during the stream crossings and in plunging dumped the men from their litters uttering anguished cries of pain.

Yet even in these straits Crook kept up the pursuit when events justified it. On the twelfth he sent Upham with 150 men of the Fifth Cavalry to reconnoiter along an Indian trail discovered the preceding night. Upham was gone for two days on limited rations and failed to find any villages. Tribesmen were close by, however. On the morning of September 14 they killed and scalped one of the major's men found hunting near the Belle Fourche River.[15] Meanwhile, the rest of Crook's expedition, after marching thirty-five miles, camped for the night of the twelfth along Willow Creek, about six miles from the Belle Fourche. Soldiers got lost after dark, and some wandered into bivouac long past midnight. Lieutenant Bourke prepared a ragout of onions, pony meat, and marrow from the shinbone of a dead beef found on the trail, but most of the men got no rations that night.[16] "Men very weak and despondent," recorded an enlisted man in his diary, "many of them unable to stand on their Feet, and some drop[p]ing to sleep on the . . . wet ground . . . with out covering of any kind."[17] Survival now became the ultimate concern. As Surgeon Clements expressed it, "They had reached the limit of human endurance."[18]

The command rested until noon the next day, letting its stragglers catch up and building a necessary corduroy before crossing Willow Creek. Then the soldiers pushed on to the Belle Fourche: "All eyes . . . strained in the direction of Deadwood," wrote Bourke, "for word had come from

Another scene staged for Morrow's camera, showing soldiers fighting over a piece of horsemeat, probably in jesting exaggeration of what actually occurred on the march. Courtesy of the W. H. Over Museum.

Mills and Bubb that they had been successful."[19] Suddenly a loud cheer escaped the men as fifty head of cattle crested the hill in front of Crook's army. A mile behind them came the ox-drawn wagons, containing bacon, flour, sugar, vegetables, crackers, butter, and eggs. The soldiers hurrahed their approach. Mills did not accompany the relief party back to meet Crook. Ill from exposure and overexertion, the captain had stayed in Crook City to rest and recuperate.[20]

With food other than horsemeat available for the first time in days, the men's spirits rose. Their ordeal was over, and, almost predictably, the sun shone—"the first fair look we had of his face for ten dreary days," remarked Bourke.[21] Welcoming committees from Crook City and Deadwood arrived too,[22] and while soldiers promptly killed and butchered the cattle, photographer Stanley J. Morrow posed some of them fighting over horsemeat to record graphically for posterity the privations sustained by General Crook's command.[23] Captain Burt described the welcome:

Citizens of Deadwood and Crook City flocked to see what they would not believe, that they would [not] be long corralled in the hills by Indians. That the relief column had actually come was incredible. They welcomed the soldiers in words and handshaking, and will repeat it in some substantial way, probably giving [them] the freedom of the cities—that is, free feeding and drinking.[24]

Not surprisingly, more and more supply wagons continued to show up from Deadwood and Crook City as word of the arrival of the army troops circulated. Before long, wrote Schwatka, "the line of sutlers' wagons seemed to convert our encampment into a big county fair." The purveyors sold their goods at enormous prices, and Schwatka reported paying three to five dollars a pound for butter and ten dollars for a bushel of potatoes. The prices suddenly dropped as more wagons arrived and the competition consequently increased, until a pound of butter could be had for only fifty cents.[25]

In the meantime, news of the victory of Slim Buttes went forth in a competitive manner. With Mills's group when it left Crook had been Frank Grouard, who was in-

Jack Crawford, the "poet" scout, who attempted to race Crook's
official emissary to the nearest telegraph line with news of the
Slim Buttes battle, but was only partly successful. Courtesy of
the Nebraska State Historical Society.

structed to carry Crook's dispatches south, and the scout
Jack Crawford, who, in collusion with correspondent Davenport, was to try to beat the official accounts of the battle
into print. As the Mills party traveled south, Crawford constantly tried to steal away to be first to reach the telegraph
line. As soon as Mills reached Crook City, Crawford and
Grouard were off. Grouard reached the line at Hat Creek,
in northwestern Nebraska, only to find it under repair. He
went on to Fort Laramie. Crawford arrived at Hat Creek
and left Davenport's dispatches to be wired as soon as
the line was restored. By the time Grouard reached Fort
Laramie, Davenport's story was being transmitted from
Hat Creek. At an appropriate pause, however, the telegra-
pher at Fort Laramie broke in with Crook's dispatches and
continued an uninterrupted transmission until he had
finished, so that only part of Davenport's account went in
before the official report.[26]

For two days the men of the Big Horn and Yellowstone
Expedition rested in bivouac by the Belle Fourche. While
the troops recovered from their travail, Second Lieutenant
Edward L. Keyes of Company C, Fifth Cavalry, was dispatched with an escort to go back to retrieve the boxes of
ammunition earlier cached along the trail and to gather up
whatever abandoned horses he found alive.[27] On the second night word reached Crook from Sheridan, announcing
the delivery of provisions to Custer City, in the southern
Black Hills, and requesting Crook's immediate presence
at Fort Laramie, where the two officers could consult personally. Sheridan was eager to concentrate Crook's soldiers at Camp Robinson to intimidate troublesome elements among the Sioux at the Red Cloud and Spotted Tail
agencies.[28] Crook responded the next day, after moving his
command to Whitewood Creek. He told Sheridan that he
would leave the next morning and "travel thirty to forty
miles a day until I reach there."[29] That evening Crook is-

Crook City, Dakota Territory, as it appeared in September, 1876. Courtesy of the Custer Battlefield National Monument.

sued instructions permitting Dr. Clements to leave some of the sick and wounded at Crook City under the care of medical personnel Clements might designate.[30]

On Saturday morning, the sixteenth, Crook and his entourage departed, leaving Colonel Merritt in charge of the troops. The general's party rode sixteen miles to Crook City, where exuberant citizens welcomed the town's namesake, firing cannon and anvils charged with gunpowder and blowing steam whistles to mark the occasion.[31] "We were all forcibly dismounted," remembered Finerty, "and led to an attack on Black Hills whiskey, which we found more formidable than either Sitting Bull or Crazy Horse."[32]

Later that day the general reached Deadwood, where he acknowledged an enthusiastic reception, while his staff, among other activities, ceremoniously panned for gold.[33] In Deadwood, Crook spoke to a throng gathered in front of the Grand Central Hotel and that evening addressed a meeting held in the McDaniels Theatre, during which he was presented a petition by Deadwood citizens urging construction of a military post in the area. The general politely declined it, explaining to the townspeople that "the Black Hills . . . are not in my department. Gen. Terry commands here. To the secretary of war your petition should be presented, not to me." He generously offered to deliver the document to Sheridan at Fort Laramie, an offer for which he was warmly applauded.[34] Crook closed his impromptu talk by asking the townsmen to honor his soldiers:

When the rank and file pass through here, . . . show that you appreciate their admirable fortitude in bearing the sufferings of a terrible march almost without a murmur, and . . . show them that they are not fighting for $13 per month, but for the cause—the proper development of our gold and other mineral resources, and of humanity. . . . Let the private soldier feel that he is remembered by our people as the real defender of his country.[35]

Crook reached Camp Robinson on September 20. Twenty-two soldiers accompanied him from there to Fort Laramie, which he reached the following day.[36]

On September 18 the army, under Merritt, moved to a beautiful clearing above Crook City called Centennial Park. Some of the newsmen and officers partook of Crook City's cultural offerings and spent the evening at the little log community theater viewing *Trodden Down, or Under Two Flags*. The next day the troops took a leisurely pace into the Black Hills. Von Luettwitz and another seriously wounded soldier remained at Crook City in the care of a junior surgeon and two men of Von Luettwitz's company.[37] At Deadwood the soldiers were warmly welcomed by the citizens, some of whom showed their esteem for Crook's men by promptly stealing horses from them. The residents "are anxious to have troops quartered for the winter in their midst," observed a newsman, "and in addition to stealing their horses, to have the oportunity of fleecing them of . . . [their] pay."[38]

On the way through the hills the soldiers passed several tiny communities, some no more than one or two shacks thrown up on a potentially lucrative mining claim and dignified with names like Elizabeth, Gayville, Golden City, Rapid City, Hill City ("a perfectly deserted burg," wrote Schwatka), and Custer City. Several soldiers contracted typhoid fever on the march through the Black Hills, and five of them died from the disease over the next several weeks. Fears grew that such sickness might spread if the troops did not soon receive proper shelter and new clothing. At Box Elder Creek supplies from Red Cloud Agency reached the troops, and at Rapid City more beef cattle and forage awaited them, having been routed around the hills from Fort Laramie.[39]

On September 23 the command arrived at Custer City, a former boomtown, where supplies from Camp Robinson awaited them.[40] In the meantime, desertions grew with the increased lure of the goldfields; between September 15 and September 27 no fewer than seventeen soldiers took French leave and left the column.[41] The rest of Merritt's army bivouacked in the hills surrounding Custer City through half of October, regaining their strength. On October 14 the Fifth Cavalry, accompanied by detachments of the Second and Third regiments, reconnoitered the south fork of the Cheyenne River to the mouth of Rapid Creek before turning back toward Custer City. During the month the troops received reinforcements, 321 recruits, most of whom went to the Fifth Cavalry. By then, however, the summer campaign was over. The whole assemblage proceeded to Camp Robinson, where General Crook on October 24 formally disbanded the Big Horn and Yellowstone Expedition.[42] He publicly extolled his men for their participation in a campaign that, he said, "has but few parallels in the history of our Army."[43] In his published farewell Crook generalized on the subject of combat with Indians:

Indian warfare is of all warfare the most dangerous, the most trying, and the most thankless. Not recognized by the high authority of the United States Congress as war, it still possesses for you the disadvantages of civilized warfare with all the horrible accompaniments that barbarism can invent and savages can execute. In it you are required to serve without the incentive to promotion or recognition—in truth, without favor or hope of reward.[44]

Despite the last statement two members of Crook's command received Medals of Honor for their action at Slim Buttes. They were Sergeant John A. Kirkwood and Private Robert Smith, both of Company M, Third Cavalry, who were rewarded for their valor while "endeavoring to dislodge Indians secreted in a ravine."[45] In addition, Captain Mills recommended brevets for Lieutenants Schwatka, Crawford, Von Luettwitz, and Bubb and medals for ten of the enlisted men who attacked "in the darkness, and in the wilderness, and on the heels of the late appalling disasters to their comrades, a village of unknown strength."[46]

While personal accolades were bestowed by the various commanders involved, Crook's campaign drew both praise and scorn from outside the military establishment. Considering that the victory over the thirty-seven-lodge hostile encampment at Slim Buttes involved nearly two thousand soldiers—the largest government force present in any of

the encounters with the Sioux and Cheyennes in 1876—
Crook had little to boast about. Too weak from hunger to
mount an offensive against either the tribesmen fleeing the
Slim Buttes village or those of neighboring camps, the
command consequently failed to punish the hostiles severely. At Slim Buttes, Crook had captured a few Sioux and
some ponies and had managed to hold the ground, but that
was all.[47] "So far the result of this expedition has been
nothing but disaster, and a depletion of the public purse,"
bemoaned a disgruntled member of the Fifth Cavalry who
had been with Crook, adding, "Custer and his 300 brave
soldiers still remain unavenged."[48] The correspondent for
the *New York Times* on the expedition recited the generally
negative feeling persisting among the troops. Writing from
Custer City on September 22, he reported that:

the general impression in this command is that we have not
much to boast of in the way of killing Indians. They kept out of
the way so effectually that the only band which was struck was
struck by accident, and when, by the subsequent attack upon us,
it was discovered that another and much larger village was not far
off, the command was in too crippled and broken down a condition from starvation and overmarching to turn the information
to any account.[49]

Much animosity was directed toward the leader of the
summer campaign. The Fifth cavalryman quoted above
fairly indicted Crook for incompetence in command:

I firmly believe . . . that there would not have been a murmur of
disaffection among the troops, had there been a shadow of a
cause for the existence of such a state of affairs; but as it was
merely to satisfy a fleeting fancy of General Crook, who was en-
dowed in the premises with discretionary and unlimited authority, the greatest discontent, want of energy, and carelessness existed in the command. I have no doubt but that more favorable
results would have been attained, and the people of the United
States would probably not be obliged to replace about 300 horses
abandoned since the 5th of August.[50]

Even Crook's staunch admirer, Lieutenant Charles King, could not contain his disappointment in the general. In a letter home he wrote:

I fear that even the 5th [Cavalry] cannot uphold their old chief as they did in Arizona [in the early 1870s]. He certainly is greatly altered and while in the 2d and 3d Cavalry & the Infantry of his command he has not a friend left, there are still two or three in the 5th who are hoping that certain things may yet be explained before they too lose respect & confidence.[51]

Such stinging personal criticism was avoided by reporters for the eastern papers, most of whom felt that Crook had done a creditable job but that the campaign had failed largely because of conditions and circumstances beyond his immediate control. Editorialized the popular *Harper's Weekly*:

The result of this summer's operations against the Sioux shows that while it is practicable to surprise and destroy Indian villages, it is almost impossible to force a battle with the Indians. Our cavalry horses seem to be no match for Indian ponies either in speed or endurance.[52]

To Crook's great credit was the fact that Slim Buttes was the only solid victory over the Sioux to date, and eastern tabloids, so accustomed to reporting military setbacks, headlined the success appropriately. "Squaw Scalps," elated the *Chicago Times*'s edition of September 17. "At Last Crook Can Make a Showing for His Summer's Work. The Net Results Being Several Indians, Two Squaws, and a 'Nit' Killed." Terming Mills's dawn assault "A Siouxprise," the paper told how "American Horse, Mortally Wounded, Gives His Views of the Sioux Situation." The *Chicago Tribune* headlined its coverage of the ravine fight with "He-Fiends, She-Fiends, and Imps Driven Into a Gulch and Mostly Killed."[53] Most of the published stories were penned by the newsmen who had been with Mills and

Crook at Slim Buttes. With few exceptions their accounts were supportive of the general's strategy in heading for the Black Hills and delivering the hostiles at least one solid blow. Wrote *Rocky Mountain News* correspondent Strahorn:

This [Slim Buttes battle] is emphatically *the* event of the campaign so far as punishment for the Indians is concerned, and the participants under General Crook deserve the lasting thanks of our people, for without a doubt the den of redskins so thoroughly rooted out has furnished shelter for more than one of the plundering savages who have annoyed us recently.[54]

John F. Finerty gave Crook high marks for perseverance:

All other commanders had withdrawn from pursuit . . . , but Crook resolved to teach the savages a lesson. He meant to show them that neither distance, bad weather, the loss of horses nor the absence of rations could deter the American army from following up its wild enemies to the bitter end.[55]

Such sentiments came easily in the afterglow of what had been an unusually arduous campaign. They also had the effect of ascribing to Crook some kind of prophetic power, a quality that he in fact had lacked at the critical juncture at Heart River, when he had made his decision to head for the Black Hills. Yet the Slim Buttes encounter provided a boost for the much-demoralized command while simultaneously ending the summer's campaign on a note of success. The tactic employed by Mills in sacking the Indian camp, used later by Colonel Mackenzie against the Northern Cheyennes and by Colonel Miles against the Sioux, contributed significantly to ending the Sioux War in the spring of 1877. Furthermore, these later commands sought to emulate Crook's method of using mule packtrains, departing from the customary wagon transportation, thereby permitting greater fluidity of movement.[56] In sum, Crook's relentless pursuit, coupled with Mills's daring strike, exemplified at its best the concept of total war as applied against the Indians, and the subsequent campaigns were a direct result.[57] From a purely military standpoint the shock of the dawn attack and the attendant ruin of their homes, food, and material goods forced the Indians to choose between the grim realities of starvation and ultimate surrender.

The impact of the Slim Buttes engagement was fully appreciated by the Tetons, and probably Crook's soldiers unwittingly prolonged hostilities by their encounter—on the reservation—with supposedly agency-bound Indians. Fearing retribution, many of the warriors now avoided the agencies altogether and returned to winter with Crazy Horse in the Powder River country. Other groups joined Sitting Bull north of the Yellowstone River and went with the Hunkpapa leader into Canada early in 1877. Some of the tribesmen already at the agencies grew alarmed by the recent military presence and fled to the hostile camps.[58]

Most threatening, however, was the prospect of starvation, either among the hostiles or at the agencies. The latest action of the United States government offered the Sioux exactly those alternatives. In its effort to gain undisputed control of the lucrative Black Hills mining area, Congress in August had passed limited appropriations for the reservation Sioux, stipulating that additional funds for food and clothing would be forthcoming only after the Indians relinquished their right to the Black Hills established by earlier treaties. Violating provisions of those accords that required the signatures of three-fourths of the adult males on the reserve to ratify such transactions, agents and commissioners joined openly to defraud the Sioux.[59] The calamity experienced by their kinsmen at Slim Buttes must have contributed to the fear and dissension among the reservation Indians. In the end they succumbed to the pressure. The Black Hills Agreement of September 26, 1876,

unlawfully stripped them of the valuable domain, which
amounted to roughly one-third of their entire reservation.[60] That blow, along with continued army harassment
through the ensuing winter, broke the hostiles' resistance,
and by May, 1877, almost 4,500 Sioux and Cheyennes,
including the previously indomitable Crazy Horse, had
laid down their arms at Red Cloud and Spotted Tail agencies.[61] Only at Wounded Knee, thirteen years later, would
the challenge of the Tetons find its resolution in perfect
tragedy.

Epilogue

THE BATTLE OF SLIM BUTTES was largely forgotten in the years after 1876. Then, in 1914, Walter M. Camp of Chicago, editor of *Railway Review* and a devoted student of the western Indian wars, became intrigued with finding the Slim Buttes battleground. Accompanied by the aged Anson Mills and retired Brigadier General Charles Morton, who had been a subaltern with Crook during the engagement, Camp went to Belle Fourche, South Dakota, and proceeded by rented automobile to Slim Buttes. The men failed to find the village site, however, and after several days of unsuccessful searching they returned to the East. Undaunted, Camp interviewed other army and Indian participants, and acquired from retired Brigadier General Charles King a detailed map of the terrain. Armed with much new information, Camp returned to South Dakota and, with the help of ranchers in the region, on June 19, 1917, established the location of the Slim Buttes battlefield. The discovery of a large number of expended .45/70 cartridges, some burned lodgepoles, broken cooking equipment, and human skeletal remains confirmed the identification of the site. The Slim Buttes battleground straddled portions of Sections 9, 10, 11, 15, and 16, Township 18 North, Range 8 East, in Harding County.[1]

On modern road maps the site adjoins South Dakota State Highway 20, 2.1 miles west of the Reva post office. Near the road stands an eight-foot-high shaft with bronze tablets memorializing the battle. The marker is actually half a mile northwest of the village site, and little of the battlefield can be seen from the highway. Former Sergeant John A. Kirkwood, who fought at Slim Buttes, helped place the monument. Mills financed the operation and, much against Camp's wishes, agreed with Kirkwood to erect the marker close to the highway so that it could be seen by travelers.[2] The marker was dedicated in August, 1920, before an assemblage of local residents. Markers for the Slim Buttes dead of Crook's command surround the base of the cast iron shaft.[3]

Anson Mills, the man whose Third Cavalry force charged the village in the morning gloom of September 9, 1876, won a brevet of colonel for his service at Slim Buttes and retired from the army a brigadier general in 1897. In 1921, forty-five years after the event, Mills applied through former Commanding General Nelson A. Miles for a Medal of Honor based on his performance in the fight. Crook had died in 1890. Mills contended that the general's "sudden death" had prevented him from receiving his just due, though fourteen years had elapsed between the encounter and Crook's passing. Existing statutes precluded his receiving the award. General Mills died at ninety on November 5, 1924, one of the last surviving officers of the Sioux War and the combat at Slim Buttes, Dakota Territory.[4]

Crook's late-summer campaign of 1876 drew both praise and controversy and created some lasting animosities. The engagements, the starvation march, and their aftermath were caustically summed up in the following literary endeavor purportedly composed soon after Slim Buttes by an unidentified officer of the Fifth Cavalry:[5]

> At Slim Butte, neath the noon-day sun,
> After the "Third" the fight had won,
> Came Crook and pack-train on the run,
>   To jump the captured property.

Marker in Harding County, South Dakota, commemorating the
Battle of Slim Buttes.

But Slim Butte saw another scene,
For close by, in a deep ravine
Two bucks and several squaws had been
    Firing with great rapidity.

'Twas then each crow-bate [*sic*] charger neighed,
And said "I'm d——d if I ain't played,"
And George Crook like a BURO [*sic*] brayed,
    Betraying his identity.

Then several faint attempts were made
To charge with Crook's blood red brigade;
But rag-cap, packer, scout and guide
    Fell back with great agility.

But greater yet will be the fight,
When some one dares the truth to write;
Of Slim Butte's bloodless dried beef fight
    And George's great absurdity.

'Twas then a squaw drew near the band,
And George advanced and seized her hand
And said "Now yield to my command
   Or sink into obscurity!"

The squaw confessed that she was beat,
And that it was a great defeat.
This nobly aided Crook's retreat
   And proved his capability.

Then rose a wild and piercing yell
That rent the air like sounds from hell.
And shots mid herds and pickets fell,
   Stampeding Crook's sagacity.

The skirmish thickens, "fight, men, fight!
One buck has fallen on the right.
Wave, George, thy flag in wild delight,
   And snort with mule stupidity."

'Tis done. The ration fight is o'er.
Two hundred purps lie sick and sore.
And ponies' flanks are gushing gore
   To stimulate humidity.

Too few are left who care to tell
How starved men fought and ponies fell;
But "Crook was right," the papers yell,
   To George's great felicity.

Appendices

APPENDIX A

Organizational Roster
The Big Horn and Yellowstone Expedition
September 9–10, 1876

The following officers and units were present for duty September 9–10, 1876, and took part in the actions at Slim Buttes, Dakota Territory. This is not a comprehensive listing of all officers who were assigned to particular units and may have been on leave or detached service.

Headquarters and Staff

Brigadier General George Crook, United States Army, Commanding

First Lieutenant John Gregory Bourke, Company L, Third Cavalry, Assistant Adjutant General

Captain Azor Howitt Nickerson, Twenty-third Infantry, Aide-de-Camp

First Lieutenant William Philo Clark, Company I, Second Cavalry, Aide-de-Camp

Second Lieutenant Walter Scribner Schuyler, Company B, Fifth Cavalry, Aide-de-Camp

Captain John Wilson Bubb, Company I, Fourth Infantry, Acting Commissary of Subsistence

Dr. Bennett Augustine Clements, Medical Director

Dr. (Major) Albert Hartsuff, Assistant Surgeon

Dr. (Captain) Julius Herman Patzki, Assistant Surgeon

Charles R. Stephens, Acting Assistant Surgeon

R. B. Grimes, Acting Assistant Surgeon

William Cooper Lecompte, Acting Assistant Surgeon

Valentine T. McGillycuddy, Acting Assistant Surgeon

Junius Levert Powell, Acting Assistant Surgeon

Captain George Morton Randall, Company I, Twenty-third Infantry, Chief of Scouts

Major Thaddeus Harlan Stanton, Paymaster, United States
Army, commanding irregulars, volunteers, civilian employees,
etc.

Cavalry Brigade

Colonel Wesley Merritt, Fifth Cavalry, Commanding

First Lieutenant William Curtis Forbush, Company K, Fifth
Cavalry, Acting Assistant Adjutant General

First Lieutenant William Preble Hall, Company E, Fifth Cavalry, Acting Assistant Adjutant General

Second Lieutenant Julius Hayden Pardee, Twenty-third Infantry,
Aide-de-Camp to Colonel Merritt

Second Lieutenant Robert Hunter Young, Fourth Infantry, Aide-
de-Camp to Colonel Merritt

Fifth Cavalry

Lieutenant Colonel Eugene Asa Carr, Commanding

First Lieutenant Charles King, Company K, Regimental Adjutant

First Battalion

Major John Jacques Upham, Commanding

Second Lieutenant Hoel Smith Bishop, Company G, Battalion
Adjutant

Company A: Captain Calbraith Perry Rodgers
Company C: Captain Emil Adam
            Second Lieutenant Edward Livingston Keyes
Company G: Captain Edward Mortimer Hayes
Company I: Captain Sanford Cobb Kellogg
            First Lieutenant Bernard Reilly, Jr.
            Second Lieutenant Robert London
            Second Lieutenant Satterlee Clark Plummer,
                Fourth Infantry, attached
Company M: Captain Edward Henry Leib

Second Battalion

Major Julius Wilmot Mason, Commanding

Second Lieutenant Charles Dyer Parkhurst, Company E, Battalion Adjutant

Company B: Captain Robert Hugh Montgomery
Company D: Captain Samuel Storrow Sumner

Company E: Captain George Frederic Price
Company F: Captain John Scott Payne
             First Lieutenant Alfred Boyce Bache
Company K: Captain Albert Emmett Woodson

Second and Third Cavalry Battalions

Lieutenant Colonel William Bedford Royall, Third Cavalry, Commanding

Battalion, Second Cavalry

Captain Henry Erastus Noyes, Company I, Commanding
Company A: Captain Thomas Bull Dewees
             Second Lieutenant Daniel C. Pearson
Company B: First Lieutenant William Charles Rawolle
Company D: First Lieutenant Samuel Miller Swigert
             Second Lieutenant Henry Dustan Huntington
Company E: Captain Elijah Revillo Wells
             Second Lieutenant Frederick William Sibley
Company I: Second Lieutenant Fred William Kingsbury

Battalion, Third Cavalry

Major Andrew Wallace Evans, Commanding
Second Lieutenant Henry Rowan Lemly, Company E, Battalion Adjutant
Company A: First Lieutenant Joseph Lawson
             Second Lieutenant Charles Morton
Company B: Captain Charles Meinhold
             Second Lieutenant James Ferdinand Simpson
Company C: Captain Frederick Van Vliet
Company D: Second Lieutenant William Wallace Robinson, Jr.
Company E: First Lieutenant Adolphus H. Von Luettwitz
Company F: First Lieutenant Alexander Dallas Bache Smead
             Second Lieutenant Bainbridge Reynolds
Company G: First Lieutenant Emmet Crawford
Company I: Captain William Howard Andrews
             First Lieutenant Albert Douglas King
             Second Lieutenant James Evans Heron Foster
Company L: Captain Peter Dumont Vroom
             Second Lieutenant George Francis Chase
Company M: Captain Anson Mills
             First Lieutenant Augustus Choteau Paul
             Second Lieutenant Frederick Schwatka

Infantry

Major Alexander Chambers, Fourth Infantry, Commanding

Fourth Infantry

Company D: First Lieutenant Henry Seton
Company F: Captain Gerhard Luke Luhn
Company G: Captain William Henry Powell
           Second Lieutenant Albert Burnley Crittenden

Ninth Infantry

Company C: Captain Samuel Munson
           First Lieutenant Thaddeus Hurlbut Capron
           Second Lieutenant Hayden De Lany
Company G: First Lieutenant William Lewis Carpenter
Company H: Captain Andrew Sheridan Burt
           Second Lieutenant Charles Mortimer Rockefeller
           Second Lieutenant Edgar Brooks Robertson

Fourteenth Infantry

Company B: Captain James Kennington
           First Lieutenant John Murphy
           Second Lieutenant Charles Frederick Lloyd
Company C: Captain Daniel Webster Burke
Company F: Captain Thomas Fry Tobey
           Second Lieutenant Frederic Sanscay Calhoun
Company I: First Lieutenant Frank Taylor
           Second Lieutenant Richard Thomas Yeatman

APPENDIX B

Casualties at Slim Buttes, Sept. 9, 1876

Unofficial Accounting

(From John F. Finerty's notebook, as contained in *War-Path and Bivouac*, pp. 342–43)

Killed

3d Cavalry, Troop A—Private John Wenzel, alias Medbury.
5th Cavalry, Troop E—Private Edward Kennedy.
Scouts and guides—Charley, alias Frank, White, alias "Buffalo Chip."

Wounded

2d Cavalry, Troop I—Private J. M. Stevenson, severely; Privates Shanahan and Walsh, slightly.
3d Cavalry, Troop E—First Lieut. A. H. Von Leutwitz [*sic*], shot through right knee joint; the limb amputated on the field.
Troop B—Private Charles Foster, hip joint shattered and amputated.
Troop C—Private William Dubois, severely, and three other soldiers, names not recorded, slightly wounded.
Troop D—Private August Dorn, severely; two men slightly wounded.
Troop E—Sergeant Edward Glass, right arm shattered, disabled for life. Private Edward McKeon severely, and privates [*sic*] Kennedy and Taggert slightly wounded.
Troop M—Sergt. Kirkwood, severely, and Private Moriarty, slightly wounded.
5th Cavalry, Troop D—Private Daniel Ford, severely, Private C. Wilson, slightly wounded.
Troop K—Private Edward Schrisher, severely, three men slightly wounded.

Slim Buttes Casua

Name	Rank	Co.	Regiment	Injury	
				Missile/Weapon	Sea
1. Fitzhenry, Robert	Pvt	H	9th Infantry	Conical bullet	L. Thig
2. Kennedy, Edward	Pvt	C	5th Cavalry	Conical bullet	R. Kne
3. Cloutier, George	Pvt	D	5th Cavalry	Conical bullet	R. Glu Regi
4. Madden, William	Pvt	M	5th Cavalry	Conical bullet	R. Leg
5. Schreiber, Edmund	Sgt	K	5th Cavalry	Conical bullet	R. Thig
6. Ford, Daniel	Pvt	F	5th Cavalry	Conical bullet	R. Hip
7. Donally, Michael	Pvt	F	5th Cavalry	Conical bullet	R. Thig
8. Von Leuttwitz [sic], A. H.	1st Lieut.	E	3rd Cavalry	Conical bullet	R. Kne
9. Dubois, William H.	Pvt	C	3rd Cavalry	Conical bullet	L. Side of H
10. Glass, Edward	Sgt	E	3rd Cavalry	Conical bullet	R. Fore
11. Foster, Charles	Pvt	D	3rd Cavalry	Conical bullet	R. Thig left l
12. McKiernan, Edward	Pvt	E	3rd Cavalry	Conical bullet	R. Thig
13. Kirkwood, John A.	Sgt	M	3rd Cavalry	Conical bullet	L. Side
14. Dorn, August	Pvt	D	3rd Cavalry	Conical bullet	R. Side of fac over
15. Stephenson, J. W.	Pvt	I	2nd Cavalry	Conical bullet	L. Foo Fract

There were several of the infantry slightly wounded, but in the confusion incident on the fight and subsequent march, their names were not ascertained. In fact, slight wounds counted for nothing at that period.

A sergeant of the 2d Cavalry, named Cornwell . . . was reported missing. It was supposed at the time that he had strayed from the column in a fit of temporary insanity, and had fallen into the hands of the Indians. A soldier named Miller [Milner], who belonged to Major Upham's battalion of the 5th Cavalry, was shot and killed by the Indians while engaged in hunting a few days after the Slim Buttes affair.

cial Accounting*

Nature	Treatment	Result	Remarks
Severe	Simple Dressings		
evere	Stimulants	Died Sept. 9th 1876	Died from shock
Severe	Simple Dressings, Extraction of ball by counter incision.		
light	Simple Dressings		Wounded on Sept. 10th 1876.
Severe	Simple Dressings		
light	Simple Dressings	Duty Sept. 12th 1876	
Severe	Simple Dressings	Duty Sept. 12th 1876	
Severe	Amputation lower third thigh	Transf'rd Sept. 17th 76	Transferred Sept. 17th 1876
Severe	Simple Dressings		
Severe	Splint and extraction of ball by incision.		
Severe	Plaster Splint from hip to ankle, and extraction of ball from hand.	Transf'rd Sept. 17th 76	Transferred Sept. 17th 1876
Severe	Simple Dressings		
Severe	Simple Dressings		
Severe	Simple Dressings		Pereosteum stripped from frontal bone.
Severe	Simple Dressings		Fracture of Metatarsal bone.

*List of wounded in the Big Horn and Yellowstone Expedition, Army of Department of the Platte, at the Action of "Slim Buttes" on a branch of the south fork of Grand River D.T. on the ninth day of September, 1876. (Source: "Surgeon's Report on the Battle of Slim Buttes, 1876." F-467. Record Group 94, National Archives.)

APPENDIX C

Official Reports of the Battle of Slim Buttes
(From *Report of the Secretary of War, 1876*)

Telegram from General Crook

Headquarters Department of the Platte,
Big Horn and Yellowstone Expedition,
Camp on Owl River, Dakota, September 10, 1876.

General Sheridan, Chicago:

Marched from Heart River, passing a great many trails of Indians going down all the different streams we crossed between Heart River and this point, apparently working their way in toward the different agencies.

Although some of the trails seemed fresh, our animals were not in condition to pursue them.

From the North Fork of Grand River, I sent Captain Mills, of the Third Cavalry, with 150 men, mounted on our strongest horses, to go in advance to Deadwood and procure supplies of provisions.

On the evening of the 8th, he discovered, near the Slim Buttes, a village of thirty-odd lodges, and lay by there that night and attacked them by surprise yesterday morning, capturing the village, some prisoners, and a number of ponies, and killing some of the Indians. Among the Indians was the chief American Horse, who died from his wounds, after surrendering to us. Our own casualties were slight, but among them was Lieutenant Von Leuttwitz [*sic*] of the Third Cavalry, wounded seriously in knee, and leg since amputated.

In the village were found, besides great quantities of dried meat and ammunition, an army guidon, portions of officers' and noncommissioned officers' uniforms, and other indications that the Indians of this village had participated in the Custer massacre.

130

Our main column got up about noon that day, and was shortly after attacked by a considerable body of Indians, who, the prisoners said, belonged to the village of Crazy Horse, who was camped somewhere between their own village and the Little Missouri River. This attack was undoubtedly made under the supposition that Captain Mills's command had received no reenforcements.

The prisoners further stated that most of the hostile Indians were now going into the agencies, with the exception of Crazy Horse and Sitting Bull with their immediate followers. Crazy Horse intended to remain near the headwaters of the Little Missouri; and about one-half of Sitting Bull's band, numbering from sixty to one hundred lodges, had gone north of the Yellowstone, while the remainder of that band, with some Sans Arcs, Minneconjous, and Uncpapas, had gone in the vicinity of Antelope Buttes, there to fatten their ponies and to trade with the Rees and others.

I place great reliance in these statements, from other corroboratory evidence which I have.

Those Indians with Sitting Bull will amount probably to three hundred or four hundred lodges, and in my judgment can very easily be struck by General Terry's column, provided it go in light marching order and keep under cover.

Our prisoners in their conversation also fully confirmed in every particular my opinions as already telegraphed you.

We had a very severe march here from Heart River eighty[-]fo[u]r consecutive miles. We did not have a particle of wood; nothing but a little dry grass, which was insufficient even to cook coffee for the men. During the greater portion of the time we were drenched by cold rains, which made traveling very heavy. A great many of the animals gave out and had to be abandoned. The others are now in such weak condition that the greater number of them will not be able to resume the campaign until after a reasonable rest.

I should like to have about five hundred horses, preferably the half-breed horses raised on the Laramie plains or in the vicinity of Denver and already acclimated to this country.

I intend to carry out the programme mentioned in my last dispatch via Fort Lincoln, and shall remain in the vicinity of Deadwood until the arrival of my wagon-train.

George Crook,
Brigadier-General.

Report of Captain Mills

Headquarters Detachment Third Cavalry,
In Bivouac on Rabbit Creek, Dakota,
September 9, 1876

Lieut. George F. Chase,
    Adjutant Battalion Third Cavalry:
    Sir: I have the honor to submit the following report of the engagement of this date between my command and a village of thirty-seven lodges, under Brulé Sioux chiefs American Horse· and Roman Nose, at Slim Buttes, Dakota Territory.
    My command consisted of four officers and 150 enlisted men, all from the Third Cavalry, save Lieutenant Bubb, Fourth Infantry, acting commissary subsistence and acting quartermaster to the general commanding the expedition, being fifteen men from each of the ten companies of the regiment serving with the expedition, selected with reference to both men and horses; one chief packer, Thomas Moore; fifteen packers, and sixty-one pack mules.
    Lieut. Emmet Crawford commanded the detachment of 75 men from Second Battalion, and Lieut. A. H. Von Luettwitz commanded the detachment of same strength from the First Battalion.
    The detachment separated from the expedition on the night of the 7th, at camp on a branch of the North Fork of Grand River, with orders to proceed as rapidly as possible to Deadwod City, in the Black Hills, for rations, the expedition being then in almost a destitute condition.
    Lieut. Frederick Schwatka was appointed adjutant to the detachment. The command marched south at 7 p.m., under the guidance of Mr. Frank Gruard [sic], chief to the guide, assisted by Captain Jack, 18 miles, and camped because of the utter darkness. Marched at daylight on the 8th through heavy rain and mud, when, at 3 p.m., the guide discovered, on the slope of Slim Buttes, some forty ponies grazing, about three miles distant. As the commanding general had instructed me to lose no opportunity to strike a village, the command was rapidly put out of sight, when I, with the guides, proceeded to ascertain, if possible, if there was a village, and its location. The approaches were so difficult, that it was impossible for us to learn anything without being discovered until dark, when I decided to move back about a mile and put the command in a deep gorge, wait there until 2

o'clock a.m., and attack at daylight. The night was one of the ugliest I ever passed—dark, cold, rainy, and muddy in the extreme. At 2 a.m. we moved to within a mile of the village, where I left the pack-train, one hundred and twenty-five horses, with twenty-five men to hold them, under the command of Lieutenant Bubb, and marched on. Crawford and Von Luettwitz, each with fifty men dismounted, and Schwatka with twenty-five men mounted, the plan being, if possible, for Crawford to close on one side of the village and Von Luettwitz on the other, when Schwatka was to charge through at the bugle's sound, drive off all the stock, when the dismounted men would close on them; but when we were within a hundred yards of the lower end of the village, which was situated on either side of a small creek called Rabbit Creek, a small herd of loose ponies stampeded and ran through the village. Gruard informed me that all chance for a total surprise was lost, when I ordered the charge sounded, and right gallantly did Schwatka with his twenty-five men execute it.

Immediately, the dismounted detachments closed on the south side and commenced firing on the Indians, who, finding themselves laced in their lodges, the leather drawn tight as a drum by the rain, had quickly cut themselves out with their knives and returned our fire, the squaws carrying the dead, wounded, and children up the opposite bluffs, leaving everything but their limited night-clothes in our possession, Schwatka having rounded up the principal part of the herd.

All this occurred about day-break. Lieutenant Von Luettwitz, while gallently [sic] cheering his men, was severely wounded at almost the first volley, grasping my arm as he fell.

I then turned my attention to getting up the pack-train and led horses, which was quite a difficult task; and Gruard informing me from trails, the action of the Indians, and other indications that he was satisfied there were other villages near, I sent two couriers to General Crook, advising what I was doing, and requesting him to hurry forward as rapidly as possible.

The Indians, as soon as they had their squaws and children in security, returned to the contest, and soon completely encompassed us with a skirmish-line, and as my command was almost entirely engaged with the wounded, the held horses, and the skirmish-line, I determined to leave the collection of the property and provisions, with which the village was rich, to the main command on its arrival.

American Horse and his family, with some wounded, had

taken refuge in a deep gorge in the village, and their dislodgment was also, from its difficulty, left to the coming re-enforcements.

The Indians were constantly creeping to points near enough to annoy our wounded, and Lieutenants Bubb and Crawford rendered themselves conspicuous in driving them each with their small mounted detachments.

The head of General Crook's column arrived at 11.30 a.m. and American Horse, mortally wounded, his family of some twelve persons, two warriors, a niece of Red Cloud, and four dead bodies were taken from the gorge; not, however, without loss.

About 5 p.m. the Indians resumed the contest with more than double their force, but were handsomely repulsed by our then strong command.

I learn from the prisoners that Crazy Horse, with the Cheyennes, a village of some three hundred lodges, was within eight or ten miles, and that the strength of the village taken consisted of about two hundred souls, one hundred of whom were warriors.

My loss was:

Killed.—Private John Winzel [sic], Company A, Third Cavalry.

Wounded.—First Lieut. A. H. Von Luettwitz, severely; Sergeant John A. Kirkwood, Company M, Third Cavalry; Sergeant Edward Glass, Company E, Third Cavalry; Private Edward Kiernan, Company E, Third Cavalry; Private William B. DuBois, Company C, Third Cavalry; Private August Doran [Dorn], Company D, Third Cavalry; Private Charles Foster, Company B, Third Cavalry.

It is impossible to estimate the enemy's loss, as they were principally carried away, although several were left on the field.

We captured a vast amount of provisions and property, over 5,500 pounds dried meat, large quantities of dried fruit, robes, ammunition, and arms, and clothing, and 175 ponies, all of which, not appropriated to the use of the command, was utterly destroyed. Among the trophies was a guidon of the Seventh Cavalry, a pair of gloves marked Colonel Keogh, 3 Seventh Cavalry horses, and many other articles recognized to have belonged to General Custer's command.

It is usual for commanding officers to call special attention to acts of distinguished courage, and I trust the extraordinary circumstances of calling on 125 men to attack, in the darkness, and in the wilderness, and on the heels of the late appalling disasters to their comrades, a village of unknown strength, and in the gal-

lant manner in which they executed everything required of them
to my entire satisfaction, will warrant me in recommending for
brevet Lieutenants Bubb, Crawford, Von Luettwitz, and Schwatka; and for medals the following enlisted men, who also appeared
to excel: Sergeant Galob Bigalski, Co. A, Third Cavalry; Sergeant
Peter Forster, Co. I, Third Cavalry; Sergeant Edward Glass, Co.
E, Third Cavalry; Sergeant W. H. Conklin, Co. G, Third Cavalry; Sergeant John A. Kirkwood, Co. M, Third Cavalry; Corporal Frank Askwell, Co. I, Third Cavalry; Corporal John Cohen,
Co. F, Third Cavalry; Corporal John D. Sanders, Co. D, Third
Cavalry; Private John Hale, Co. C, Third Cavalry; Private Ed-
ward McKiernan, Company E, Third Cavalry; Private William
B. DuBois, Co. C, Third Cavalry; Private Robert Smith, Co. M,
Third Cavalry; also Mr. Thomas Moore, chief packer.

I am, sir, very respectfully, your obedient servant,
                              Anson Mills,
                              Captain Third Cavalry, Commanding
                              Detachment.

Indorsement

Headquarters Battalions Second and Third Cavalry
Camp on Whitewood Creek, Dakota,
September 15, 1876.
Respectfully forwarded. Captain Mills' report is supplemented as
follows: My command, composed of two battalions of the Third
Cavalry and one of the Second, arrived at the site of the Indian
village after the engagement, but Private John M. Stevenson,
Co. I, Second Cavalry, having responded when a call for volunteers was made to dislodge wounded Indians from a ravine, he
was severely wounded in the left foot. Lieutenant Von Luettwitz
subsequently lost his right leg by amputation. During the afternoon an attack upon the camp was made by Indians in increased
force, and a skirmish-line established, which successfully resisted
for several hours and repulsed the same. On the morning of the
10th instant, a desultory firing was maintained by the Sioux until
after my command, under the instructions of the chief of cavalry,
had left camp in charge of the pack-train. To cover this movement, Company I, Second Cavalry, commanded by Lieut. F. W.
Kingsbury, was, for a short time, detached.
                              W. B. Royall,
                              Lieutenant-Colonel Third Cavalry,
                              Commanding Battalions Second and
                              Third Cavalry.

Report of Lieut. Col. E. A. Carr
Operations of Fifth Cavalry near Slim Buttes, Dakota
Headquarters Fifth Cavalry,
Camp on Whitewood Creek, Dakota,
September 15, 1876.

Sir: I have the honor to submit the following report of the operations of this regiment on the 9th and 10th instants.

On the morning of the 9th instant, soon after leaving camp, I was directed to drop out of the regiment all the men with horses not able to go rapidly for seventeen miles, placing them in charge of an officer, and with the remainder proceed with the brevet major-general commanding the cavalry to the scene of Mills's engagement.

I marched with about 250 men and 17 officers, and we arrived at the village near Slim Buttes at 11.30 a.m., finding it in possession of our troops, and the command was bivouaced [sic], this regiment in the right front as we marched. But there was still a number of Indians intrenched in a rifle-pit, and in the attempts to get them out we lost one private and one scout killed.

About 4 p.m., after the whole regiment had arrived, the pickets gave the alarm of "Indians!" when I sounded "To arms!" and "Forward!" and the companies formed and marched out beyond the horses very promptly and handsomely.

The horses of Company B stampeded and went outside the line, followed by parts of others, but were skilfully brought round by the herders, under the lead of Corporal J. S. Clanton, Company B, Fifth Cavalry. The companies remained in their positions firing at the Indians, who were circling round and crawling behind ridges and firing at us, till the infantry advanced on the left flank, driving them around to the right, when the battalion commanders advanced their battalions to the right, and the Indians were driven up and over the pass at the head of the valley and out of sight.

Next morning (10th) the Indians again appeared. The companies were sent out and engaged them, and when the time for marching arrived, by direction of General Merritt, they saddled by detachments, still holding the hills on the right of the infantry. I was ordered to place one battalion on the right, relieving the infantry skirmishers, and one in rear of the village, and for the regiment to form the rear guard on the day's march.

Upham's battalion was placed on the ridge in rear of camp, and Mason's on the right.

In this operation it was necessary to withdraw Upham's battalion under fire and replace it with part of Mason's, as well as to relieve the infantry skirmishers also under fire.

I was also ordered by General Merritt to release, upon leaving the site of the village, the squaws and children in our hands, and to see that all property was effectually destroyed, both of which orders were carried out.

After the column was well under way, I directed the battalion commanders to withdraw and follow, which was done slowly from ridge to ridge, the Indians following and pressing quite boldly till we were about two miles from camp.

Our loss in the two engagements was as follows:

Killed—1. Private J. W. Kennedy, Company C, Fifth Cavalry; 2. Scout Jonathan White.

Wounded—1. Sergeant Lucifer Schreiber, Company K; 2. Trumpeter Michael Donnelly, Company F; 3. Private Daniel Ford, Company F; 4. Private George Clotier, Company D; 5. Private William Madden, Company M.

The horses which made the rapid march were much jaded, the ground being very soft and slippery, and we lost about fifteen horses, unable to travel.

The officers and soldiers behaved with their usual courage and coolness.

The officers present, besides the colonel, Bvt. Maj. Gen. Wesley Merritt, commanding all the calvary [*sic*], were:

Battalion commanders.—Maj. J. J. Upham, Fifth Cavalry; Capt. J. W. Mason, Fifth Cavalry.

Company officers.—1. Capt. Edward Leib, Company M; 2. Capt. Samuel S. Sumner, Company D; 3. Capt. Emil Adam, Company C; 4. Capt. Robert Montgomery, Company B; 5. Capt. Sanford C. Kellogg; Company I; 6. Capt. George F. Price, Company E; 7. Capt. Edward M. Hayes, Company G; 8. Capt. J. Scott Payne, Company F; 9. Capt. Albert E. Woodson, Company K; 10. Capt. Calbraith P. Rodgers, Company A.

1. Lieut. Alfred B. Bache, sick in hospital in camp, under fire; 2. Lieut. Bernard Reilly, jr.; 3. Lieut. W. C. Forbush, Acting Assistant Adjutant-General, cavalry command, present, under fire; 4. Lieut. Charles King, acting regimental adjutant; 5. Lieut. William P. Hall, acting assistant quartermaster cavalry command, present, under fire; 6. Lieut. Charles D. Parkhurst, battalion adjutant, Second Batallion [*sic*]; 7. Lieut. Edward L. Keyes; 8. Lieut. Robert London; 9. Lieut. Noel [*sic*] S. Bishop,

battalion adjutant, First Battalion; 10. Lieut. S. C. Plummer, Fourth Infantry, attached to Company I, and Acting Assistant Surgeon J. L. Powell, of Richmond, Va.

Private Patrick Nihil, Company F, shot an Indian from his saddle and got his pony.

According to the best and most reliable accounts we killed and wounded as many as seven or eight Indians.

I would add to this report, that on the 12th instant Major Upham was ordered, with 150 of the best mounted men of the regiment, to follow a trail leading down Avol Creek. He returned on the 14th, p.m., not having found a village. His men had no rations whatever, except about two ounces of dried buffalo-meat and one-fourth ounce of coffee per man, and what horse-meat the men had saved from the night before starting. It rained most of the time, making them constantly wet, and the ground very heavy and sticky, and they were without wood for two nights. Upon their return they were the worst tired men I ever saw. One of his men, Private Cyrus B. Milner, Company A, while out hunting from camp on Belle Fourche, was killed by two Indians, who approached him stealthily. The whole of his scalp was taken off, his throat cut from ear to ear, and his breast gashed. His horse was killed.

Very respectfully, your obedient servant,

E. A. Carr,

Lieutenant-Colonel Fifth Cavalry, Commanding Regiment.
Acting Assistant Adjutant-General,
Headquarters Cavalry Command,
Big Horn and Yellowstone Expedition,
Camp on Whitewood Creek, Dakota.

Report of Major Chambers

Headquarters Principal Depot General Recruiting Service,
Fort Columbus, New York Harbor,
November, 1876.

Sir: I have the honor to make the following report of the disposition of the troops of the infantry battalion on the afternoon of the 9th and morning of the 10th of September, 1876, at Slim Buttes, on Rabbit Creek, Dakota Territory.

Four companies—F, Capt. G. L. Luhn; D, First Lieut. Henry Seton, Fourth; H, Ninth, Second Lieut. Charles M. Rockefeller, and C, Fourteenth Infantry, Capt. D. W. Burke—under command of Capt. A. S. Burt, Ninth Infantry, took the commanding hills and bluffs to the south and southwest of the camp, driving away the Indians who were annoying the camp by a desultory fire at long range. This movement was made without causalty [sic], with the exception of private [sic] Robert Fitz Henry, Company H, Ninth Infantry, slightly wounded.

Companies B, Capt. J. Kennington; F, Capt. Thomas F. Tobey, and I, First Lieut. Frank Taylor, Fourteenth Infantry, were posted on the south side of camp, concealed by bluffs, ready in case an attack should be made from that direction.

Companies C, Capt. Samuel Munson, and G, First Lieut. William L. Carpenter, Ninth Infantry, took a range of bluffs on north side of camp, driving away the Indians.

Company G, Fourth Infantry, Capt. William H. Powell, reported to General Crook to perform the duty of a complete destruction of the village.

These companies having performed the duties assigned them, were withdrawn after dark, and strong pickets posted.

Before daylight on the morning of the 10th, Capt. William H. Powell, with Company G, Fourth, and B, F, and I, Fourteenth Infantry, under their respective commanders, were moved to and occupied a strong position on the bluffs south and southwest of camp, skirmishing with Indians after daylight till the whole command was under march, when they joined the infantry battalion.

The report is made at this late day, owing to subreports having been lost and but recently found.

The officers and men of the command performed their duties in their usual gallant manner.

Attention is called to the inclosed subreports.

I am, sir, very respectfully, your obedient servant,

Alex. Chamber,

Major Fourth Infantry, Commanding Infantry Battalion.

The Assistant Adjutant-General,

Big Horn and Yellowstone Expedition, Omaha, Nebr.

APPENDIX D

Discovery of the Lost Site of the Slim Buttes Battle
By Walter M. Camp
(From *South Dakota Historical Collections*, IX, 1918. Used
with permission of the South Dakota State Historical Society.)

For many years the writer has devoted recreation time to a
study of the Indian campaigns of the West, and a most interesting
part of this research has been an effort to locate or identify the
sites of some of the battlefields that have been lost. I use the
term "lost" in the historical sense of course, for while it is pre-
sumable that knowledge of all of these historic points exists in the
minds of white or Indian survivors, in the way of recollection of
landscape features, yet the fact remains that many important military engagements took place on ground that is now unknown either to the general public or to settlers of the locality; and it has
often happened that surviving eye witnesses of an event, who
have returned in after years to visit the ground upon which it occurred, have found difficulty in identifying the place.

A good illustration of such an experience may be cited in the
case of the Beecher Island fight, on the Arickaree river, in Colorado, where Lieutenant [Major] George A. Forsythe and fifty
scouts, in September, 1868, held out in that famous siege of nine
days against a superior force of Indians who had surrounded
them. For thirty years no survivor of that battle visited that part
of the country and the site became lost to public knowledge,
when finally a party of three of the survivors did try to make the
discovery, in 1898, and spent several days in a vain effort, passing
over the site without recognizing it. By mere chance they were
directed to an early settler who ten years earlier had found some
debris, which, however, he had not thought to have been connected with a battle. Under his guidance they were led to the

spot, where, after some meditation and exchange of recollections, the associations of their conceptions of the place returned
to them.

I could refer to other instances of similar searches that are
equally striking as to the difficulty, or failure, of the discovery of
historic ground. Many of the battles of these Indian campaigns
were fought long in advance of the settlement of the country, before maps had come into existence; and weather and time have
obscured evidences that would bear significance to the thing
sought.

In the case of the Battle of Slim Buttes, fought September 9,
1876, it seems to have been even more than thirty years before
any one made much of an effort to discover the site of it.

Slim Buttes, a long range of clay hills in Harding county, South
Dakota, is still far removed from railroads. The eastern slope is
well covered with grass and not a little timber. Much of the territory is now in the forest reserve. Cattle men began to range their
stock in these buttes as early as 1886 and the homesteader came
about 1905 or later, yet none of the people first in the country
pretended to have been able to locate the site of the battle that
was known to have been fought somewhere on the east side of
the Buttes.

In 1907 the writer interviewed Sioux Indians of the Standing
Rock Reservation regarding the battle, and the next year started
for the Slim Buttes country to look for the site. I proceeded as
far as Bixby, by stage, but there was unable to secure further
transportation of any kind, public or private, and was therefore
obliged to abandon the trip.

A supposed location of the site, as published in Vol. 6, State
Historical Collections, was a spot tight in the northwest corner of
Section 27, Township 17 north, Range 8 east. This point lay in the
garden of Mr. E. W. Laisy, in front of his stone residence, which
is the post office at Gill (This residence, however, is just over the
line in section 28). This garden patch, or supposed site of the battle, lies on a small wet-weather stream known as Jones Creek, a
tributary of Beaver Creek, which in turn is a tributary of Rabbit
creek. All three streams are within compass of half a mile, flowing east, and Jones Creek is the northernmost.

The Captain, Anson Mills, of 1876, who commanded the troops
in the attack on the village (Battle of Slim Buttes) is now Brigadier General, U.S. Army, retired, and is 83 years of age. About
five years ago he heard of the supposed discovery of the site of

the battle and became desirous of visiting the place to see if the point selected corresponded with his recollections of the topography. Accordingly, in July, 1914, in company with General Charles Morton, a survivor of the battle; a representative of the State Historical Society in the person of Mr. Harry A. Robinson, a son of Doane Robinson, secretary of the Society, and myself, Gen. Mills went to Slim Buttes, by automobile from Belle Fourche, and visited the ground referred to (Sec. 27-17-8). Much to his disappointment, he found that the site selected was not the one where the battle was fought. Both he and General Morton declared that the true site had not been identified, and they began to search in other localities, when, through a misunderstanding about the length of time for which the automobile had been hired, the trip was suddenly abandoned and the party returned to Belle Fourche, a distance, as the road goes, of about 130 miles.

It was then the intention to continue the search the next year, but this was not done. Gen. Charles King, another survivor of the battle, in 1915, learning that a detailed map showing the supposed location of the site had been published, declared that the location at Laisy's was wrong, and suggested that a careful search be made about 1½ miles to the southeast of said Section 27. His idea as to this proposed substitution was gained from a study of the hills shown in the Jacobson [Jacobsen] maps.

In 1915 I planned to visit the Buttes that year, with a Sioux Indian survivor of the battle, but, by reason of governmental red tape about granting permission to take the Indian off the reservation, had to abandon the trip. In the meantime, I continued my study of the location of the battle. In addition to data and sketches furnished by General Mills and Morton (the latter of whom died in 1915), I had notes from interviews with Gen. Geo. F. Chase, Gen. John W. Bubb and Gen. Charles King, besides more Sioux Indians and several enlisted men, all survivors of the battle. Gen. King sketched for me a map showing the topography of the site of the village and contiguous territory, in considerable detail. Being the engineering officer of the expedition at the time of the battle it is not necessary to comment on his qualification for this.

With these data and maps I again proceeded to the Slim Buttes country, arriving at Gill on June 16, 1917. I spent two days in that vicinity, in a careful search of the courses of Rabbit, Beaver and Jones creeks. In these investigations I had the able assistance of Mr. Laisy, above mentioned, and Mr. Louis Jones, both old residents and quite familiar with all that part of the country. Particular study was made of the landscape 1½ miles to the southeast of Gill, and round about, as directed by Gen. King; and in the opposite direction we rode to the very sources of Beaver creek and of the main Rabbit creek; but the most painstaking search failed to disclose any evidence of fighting ground. Gen. Mills had insisted that the site, wherever found, should yield broken utensils of an Indian village, empty cartridge shells and the entrenchments which he had dug for anticipated defense.

Giving up the idea that the battle could have been fought anywhere on the creeks above named, I next explored, in succession, the creeks to the north, and finally arrived at Reva Gap, where Mr. W. W. Mitchell told me of having found numerous cartridge shells on three buttes. I at once visited this ground and was able to confirm this information by finding empty shells lying promiscuously about, myself.

It being recorded that the hottest firing had occurred in driving the Indians from a butte about ¾ mile to the southwest of the village, I assumed one of these to have been that butte, and started in there and followed a northeast course to the creek bottom. Coming upon fragments of an iron tea kettle, I was gratified to discover that all of the surrounding landmarks conformed splendidly to Gen. King's map, so a minute search in the grass was begun right there.

In the party with me (on June 19) were Mr. W. W. Mitchell; his son, Earl Mitchell; Mr. Ephriam [Ephraim] Gray and Mr. Edward [Edgar] P. Coffield. A search of two and a half hours brought forth unmistakable evidence of a destroyed village, as no less than twenty-one kinds of implements or articles used by these people in their camps were picked up. In most cases the articles were nearly covered with dirt or overgrown with sod. Following is a list of some of the things found:

79 empty government cartridge shells, calibre .45-70.
Numerous pieces of partially burned tepee poles.
3 broken iron tea kettles.
Several coffee pots.
3 smashed and hacked galvanized water buckets.
Tin pans, basins, cups and cans.
Broken butcher knife.
Iron parts of a riding saddle tree.
Wooden hook of a pack saddle cinch.
Stone pestle.

An Indian stone hammer or war club.

Arrow points.

Bullets washed from a side coulee corresponding to the one where the Indians were besieged.

Broken earthenware dishes.

Broken and melted glass bottles.

Top of a canteen.

Clothes buttons.

Numerous iron hooks and handles of 5-gallon water kegs.

The tinware in all cases was crumpled up, as though done under foot, and then punctured with knives or gashed with axes, as the soldiers made a clean job of destroying the village and rendering unserviceable to the Indians every utensil in it. These broken-up articles were found scattered over a plat about 60 rods long, between extremities, where stood the thirty-seven tepees of the village, and on ground delineated precisely by the maps in hand. The star [north] fork of the stream, the gully where the Indians took refuge, and the rifle pits, all of which Gen. Mills had eagerly sought in 1914, were readily located.

At the time of the battle Gen. Mills was unaware of his location until told by captured squaws that they were on Rabbit Lip (Mashtincha Putin) creek, on the east of Slim Buttes. Gap Creek, where the discovery has been made, is one of three main branches of the "Rabbit Lip" creek of the Indians, the other two being the streams now known as Antelope and Rabbit creeks by the settlers.

With Indians it is customary to call main branches of a stream by the same name, and then, for purposes of identity, to use a qualifying word to indicate a particular tributary referred to, such as the north branch, south branch, etc. In this case, Gap creek is the north branch of Rabbit creek. The stream now called Rabbit creek is the central branch, and rises high up in the buttes. It flows eastward about ½ mile south of Gill postoffice, the distance from there to the site of the battle, on Gap creek, almost due north, being 8½ miles.

The place now known as the site of the battle to a certainty is on land owned by Mr. Earl Mitchell, in Section 10, Township 18 north, Range 8 east, in Harding county. Part of the relics found were sent to Gen. Mills, who lives in Washington, D.C. The larger portion, however, were deposited with Mr. W. W. Mitchell, as custodian, and a museum of the battle was started within a mile of the place where it was fought. As cartridge shells and debris of the destroyed village lie scattered through the grass, or lightly covered by the soil, in plenty, there is every opportunity of adding to the collection of relics already started. None of the ground occupied by the village or fought over by Crook's soldiers on the day in question has yet been plowed, although the larger portion of it is susceptible to cultivation.

One thing which has rendered this site elusive to discovery is the fact that it lies out in the open country, quite three miles from the main range of buttes, which run around it in a sort of semi circle. The ground in the neighborhood of the site of the battle is ordinary rolling prairie, with no distinctive landmarks close by. Gen. Morton had told me, when I first met him, in 1913, that one would never suspect, from the surroundings, that he was in the vicinity of the place until he would "run right onto it," and this observation proved to be correct.

To the south and southwest of the site of the village, a little more than ½ mile distant, are three small buttes, perhaps 50 to 75 feet high above the plain, and farther on in the same direction are more buttes in succession; and the country becomes more broken as the main range of the buttes is approached.

It is singular enough that in 1914 Gen. Mills and his party, under the guidance of the same W. W. Mitchell above referred to, drove over a part of this battlefield without recognizing the place. As a matter of fact we then passed between the "butte to the southwest" and the site of the village, less than ½ mile from the latter. At that time the presence of empty government cartridge shells lying all about the ground we were on seems to have been unknown to Mr. Mitchell, who had then been living in the country about 16 years. The only thing suggesting a fight that he called to our attention was an earthwork ring, about a rod in diameter such as buffalo hunters sometimes threw up around an over-night camp. This was examined by the General and dismissed as without significance to our investigation. Owing to the chauffeur's haste to start back to Belle Fourche (the particular attraction, as we afterward learned, being a base ball game at Deadwood) no further search was carefully made. We had spent the night before at Mr. Mitchell's house, only ⅝ mile southeast of the site of the village, and the two survivors of the battle present (General Mills and Morton) had talked over with our host the incidents of the battle and the landmarks, in a good deal of detail. About the most surprised man of all, therefore, when the discov-

ery was made three years later, was Mr. Mitchell, who declared
that he had ridden the range over all this ground, perhaps a hundred times, without having discovered any of the destroyed Indian property.

As soon as the village site had been identified Mr. Mitchell recalled that the remains of a human skeleton had been found on
top of a little knoll, on the south side of the creek, opposite the
village, and only about ¼ mile distant from it. This he had discovered about 18 years previously and the matter had passed out
of his recollection. Lying under the skeleton, at that time, was a
burned and bent carbine barrel, which he took possession of and
in later years had cut in two pieces and used as pins to fasten the
gates of a stock corral.

He at once invited me to visit the spot, and there, on a little
eminence just above the creek, still lay all the remains except for
the skull, and not much scattered. A light sod had grown up
through the pile of bones, and under them we found three empty
government cartridge shells. On a companion knoll, near the
creek, and only 25 or 30 rods to the west of these remains, I soon
afterward ran upon the remains of another skeleton, in much the
same condition as the one just referred to. As the gun barrel and
the empty shells found with the first seemed to me to suggest
"medicine," I proposed that we look for evidence of opened
graves, and this we soon found near the west edge of the village
site on a low bench from the creek bottom, under a clump of
buck brush that had grown up on the two mounds of earth that
had been thrown out with the excavations. These two holes in
the ground were three feet apart, and digging down, we found
solid bottom at a depth of 3½ feet. Evidently the excavations had
been made to that depth at some time. The dirt thrown out had
been weather-beaten down into flattened heaps, and enough of it
had been washed back into the two trench-like openings to fill
them within two feet of the general ground surface.

From subsequent inquiries of survivors of the battle I have
learned that the location of these excavations is about at the place
where were buried the bodies of the two soldiers (John Wenzel
and Edward Kennedy) and of the scout (Charles White) killed in
the fight; and although the precaution was taken to march the
whole cavalry command over the graves the morning that Crook
left the place, in order to trample out any appearance of freshly
dug earth, I am, from the evidence, led to inquire whether the
Indians, who returned to the village to look for their own dead,

might not have dug up these bodies, dragged them up to the two little hills, and had dances around them. It is not supposable that these could be the remains of Indians killed in battle. Can it be, therefore, that the bones of the killed on the victorious side have been bleaching in the sunlight all these years?

General Crook camped on the battlefield the night after the fight, and the next day proceeded on toward the southwest. After proceeding about 12 miles he went into camp, at 2 p.m., on September 10, on ground now occupied by the residence of Louis Jones. This is on a little stream flowing north, in a park-like vale or pass through the Buttes. About a mile south of the Jones residence and less than ½ mile west was an old Indian trail leading down the west side of the Buttes from the end of the pass, and this is the route on which the command passed through the Buttes.

The origin of the name "Slim Buttes" is a question of some interest to settlers of the locality, and many seem inclined to the opinion that it was derived from the pinnacle-like formation of many of the clay peaks to be found in the range. In and around Reva Gap, in plain view from the battlefield, the formation is striking and the scenery most picturesque. Finerty described it as resembling "a series of mammoth Norman castles, or a semi-circular range of gigantic exposition buildings." Here is really one of the most beautiful parks in the West, and it deserves to be better known.

A few miles southeast of Gill postoffice, on the eastward slope of the Buttes, stands a high, slender shaft of weathering clay or soft rock, which the settlers have named "Slim Butte," and some have supposed that this may have given the name to the whole range. From the Sioux, however, I have learned that this noted landmark was called by them "Stump Butte," as it does bear a close resemblance, in proportions and general appearance, to the stump of a tree.

The name Slim Buttes is of Indian origin. The Sioux call the range "Paha Zizipela," which means thin butte, thin (or slim) in the horizontal sense, like a snake, rather than vertically, as many of the peaks and spires really are. In other words, the thought in the mind of the Indian dwelt upon the fact that the range is very long in proportion to its width—some 45 or 50 miles in length and in most places less than three or four miles in width. The Indian name refers to the whole range as one long, slender butte, which looks slim when properly drawn on a map.

NOTES

Chapter 1

1. Theophilus F. Rodenbough, *Uncle Sam's Medal of Honor*, pp. 305–306; 312–15. Other couriers sent by Terry arrived in Crook's camp several days later. *Ibid.*, p. 316.

2. The most thorough treatment of the Powder River encounter is in J. W. Vaughn, *The Reynolds Campaign on Powder River*. Actually most of the Oglala Sioux sought by Reynolds were camped on a tributary of Little Powder River, although some were in the Cheyenne village. Mari Sandoz, *Crazy Horse, the Strange Man of the Oglalas*, p. 304; Thomas B. Marquis, *Wooden Leg: A Warrior Who Fought Custer*, p. 167.

3. The Rosebud encounter is detailed in J. W. Vaughn, *With Crook at the Rosebud*.

4. The best single volume on the Custer fight is Edgar I. Stewart, *Custer's Luck*. Evidence of Custer's planned attack at dawn on June 26 is presented in William A. Graham, ed., *The Custer Myth*, p. 33.

5. *Bismarck Tribune*, July 12, 1876, quoted in Henry E. Fritz, *The Movement for Indian Assimilation, 1860–1890*, p. 176.

6. July 12, 1876.

7. James D. Richardson, ed., *A Compilation of the Messages and Papers of the Presidents, 1789–1908*, 7:376, 407. Congress also enacted legislation forbidding conveyance to the hostiles of all forms of "metallic ammunition." *Ibid.*, pp. 398–99. Earlier proposals for troop increases included some for raising volunteers from the states and territories most directly affected by the hostilities. *New York Times*, July 8, 1876. An interesting aside on the military strength question concerned the application of a large number of Marine Corps officers to raise a battalion of marines for duty on the plains. Although General Sherman reportedly expressed interest in the idea, the upsurge of army enlistments precluded serious consideration of it. *Daily Inter-Ocean* (Chicago), August 25, 1876.

SLIM BUTTES, 1876

8. "Report of the General of the Army," November 10, 1876, in *Report of the Secretary of War, 1876*, p. 35. Hereafter cited as "Sherman's Report," November 10, 1876; *Record of Engagements with Hostile Indians Within the Military Division of the Missouri from 1868 to 1882*, p. 58.

9. George E. Hyde, *Red Cloud's Folk: A History of the Oglala Sioux Indians*, p. 278; Sheridan to Lieutenant Colonel Robert Williams, July 26, 1876, Letters Received by the Office of Indian Affairs, Dakota Superintendency, 1876, National Archives, Record Group 75. Hereafter cited as LR, Dakota Superintendency.

10. Sheridan to Williams, July 26, 1876. LR, Dakota Superintendency.

11. "Sherman's Report," November 10, 1876, pp. 35–36.

12. *Record of Engagements*, pp. 58–59.

13. Hyde, *Red Cloud's Folk*, p. 274; George E. Hyde, *Spotted Tail's Folk: A History of the Brulé Sioux*, p. 225; Stanley Vestal, *Sitting Bull, Champion of the Sioux*, p. 183; John G. Neihardt, *Black Elk Speaks: Being the Life Story of a Holy Man of the Oglala Sioux*, pp. 135, 136, 137,; Sandoz, *Crazy Horse*, p. 339.

14. Hyde, *Red Cloud's Folk*, pp. 274–75; Sandoz, *Crazy Horse*, p. 339; Neihardt, *Black Elk Speaks*, p. 135; Hyde, *Spotted Tail's Folk*, p. 225. For the post-Custer fight migrations of the Northern Cheyennes see Thomas B. Marquis, *Wooden Leg*.

15. George Crook, *General George Crook: His Autobiography*, ed. Martin F. Schmitt, p. 212. Hereafter cited as *Autobiography*.

16. "Report of Lieutenant General Sheridan," November 25, 1876, in *Report of the Secretary of War, 1876*, p. 447. Hereafter cited as "Sheridan's Report," November 25, 1876.

17. Telegram, Sheridan to General William T. Sherman, July 30, 1876, LR, Dakota Superintendency.

18. Crook, *Autobiography*, p. 200; James T. King, "General Crook at Camp Cloud Peak: 'I am at a Loss What to Do,'" *Journal of the West* 11 (January, 1972):121, 123, 124.

19. Crook, *Autobiography*, p. 200.

20. *Ellis County Star* (Hays, Kansas), October 12, 1876. See William A. Dobak, "Yellow-Leg Journalists: Enlisted Men as Newspaper Reporters in the Sioux Campaign, 1876," *Journal of the West* 13 (January, 1974):86–112.

21. Crook, *Autobiography*, p. 200; King, "General Crook at Camp Cloud Peak," p. 125.

22. Virginia Cole Trenholm and Maurine Carley, *The Shoshonis: Sentinels of the Rockies*, p. 257.

23. *Chicago Times*, September 22, 1876.

24. Crook, *Autobiography*, p. 200.

25. Oliver Knight, *Following the Indian Wars: The Story of the Newspaper Correspondents Among the Indian Campaigners*, pp. 251–52; Crook, *Autobiography*, p. 200; Peter Rosen, *Pa-Ha-Sa-Pah, or the Black Hills of South Dakota*, p. 405; Bennett A. Clements, "Report of the Medical Department of the Big Horn and Yellowstone Expedition of 1876, from August 4th to October 24th," Record Group 94, National Archives. Hereafter cited as "Medical Report." No field officers of the Second Cavalry were on duty with the five companies with Crook. See Francis B. Taunton, "Army Failures Against the Sioux in 1876," *English Westerners' Brand Book* 5 (April, 1963):6. The brief account of one of the civilian volunteers in the 1876 campaign is in W. T. Hamilton, *My Sixty Years on the Plains: Trapping, Trading, and Indian Fighting*, pp. 183–84. An organizational roster of the expedition appears in Appendix A.

26. *Inyo Independent* (Independence, Calif.), September 2, 1871.

27. Merritt's career is summarized in Mark M. Boatner III, *The Civil War Dictionary*, pp. 544–45.

28. The definitive work on Carr is James T. King, *War Eagle: A Life of General E. A. Carr.*

29. For more information on Grouard see Joe DeBarthe, *Life and Adventures of Frank Grouard*, ed. Edgar I. Stewart. The best full-length biography of Cody is in Don Russell, *The Lives and Legends of Buffalo Bill.* Biographical data on King appear in Don Russell's introduction to King's *Campaigning with Crook* and in Oliver Knight, *Life and Manners in the Frontier Army.* Two recent treatments of Bourke are in William Gardner Bell, *John Gregory Bourke: A Soldier-Scientist on the Frontier;* and John A. Turcheneske, Jr., "John G. Bourke: Troubled Scientist," *Journal of Arizona History* 20 (Autumn, 1979):323–44.

30. The conduct of the recent Rosebud fight had also caused bad feelings between Crook and some of the Third Cavalry officers. See Crook, *Autobiography*, p. 196.

31. *Chicago Times*, September 22, 1876; Crook, *Autobiography*, p. 200; Clements, "Medical Report," p. 2. One report stated that each man was limited to a two-thirds ration over a ten-day period because the number of transport animals did not proportionately increase with the reinforcements to Crook's command. *New York Times*, September 28, 1876.

32. For descriptions of 1876 cavalry dress and accouterments, see James S. Hutchins, *Boots and Saddles at the Little Bighorn.*

33. *Chicago Times*, September 22, 1876.

Chapter 2

1. *Chicago Times*, September 22, 1876.

2. *Ibid.*

3. *Ibid.*

4. *Ibid.*

5. "Sherman's Report," November 10, 1876, p. 36; *Chicago Times*, September 22, 1876.

6. *Chicago Times*, September 22, 1876.

7. *Ibid.* Finerty's prediction has been realized. In the 1970s southeastern Montana became one of the most intensively worked coal regions in the United States.

8. *Ibid.*; John G. Bourke, *On the Border with Crook*, p. 350.

9. Andrew Burt, "Account of Slim Buttes," Andrew Burt Papers, U.S. Army Military History Institute, Carlisle Barracks, Pa.

10. *Chicago Times*, September 22, 1876.

11. *Ibid.*

12. *Ibid.*

13. "Subreport of General Crook," September 25, 1876, in *Report of the Secretary of War, 1876*, p. 508. Hereafter cited as "Crook's Report," September 25, 1876; John F. Finerty, *War-Path and Bivouac; or, the Conquest of the Sioux*, p. 165; *Chicago Times*, September 22, 1876; Edward J. McClernand, "The Second Regiment of Cavalry," *Journal of the Military Institution of the United States* 13 (1892):638.

14. John Gibbon, *Gibbon on the Sioux Campaign of 1876*, p. 54.

15. *Chicago Times*, September 22, 1876.

16. The officer was Second Lieutenant Frederick Schwatka, who wrote an account of Crook's expedition for the *Daily Inter-Ocean* (Chicago). See issue of September 26, 1876.

17. *Chicago Times*, September 22, 1876.

18. *Daily Inter-Ocean*, September 26, 1876.

19. *Ibid.*; "Crook's Report," September 25, 1876; "Report of General Terry," November 21, 1876, in *Report of the Secretary of War, 1876*, p. 466. Hereafter cited as "Terry's Report," November 21, 1876.

20. "Terry's Report," November 21, 1876, p. 466.

21. *Ibid.*; "Crook's Report," September 25, 1876, p. 508; James T. King, "Needed: A Re-Evaluation of General George Crook," *Nebraska History* 45 (September, 1964):223–35; Finerty, *War-Path and Bivouac*, p. 175; Russell, *Lives and Legends of Buffalo Bill*, pp. 246–47.

22. *Chicago Tribune*, September 22, 1876.

23. Quoted in Harry H. Anderson, "Charles King's *Campaigning*

with Crook: A New and Personal Version Revealed in Family Letters," *Chicago Westerners' Brand Book* 32 (January, 1976):66.

24. Finerty, *War-Path and Bivouac*, pp. 174–75; Trenholm and Carley, *The Shoshonis*, p. 258. These Indians left Crook on August 20. Lieutenant Walter S. Schuyler to his father, November 1, 1876, in Crook, *Autobiography*, p. 204. Crook was unsuccessful in an attempt to recruit some of Gibbon's Crow scouts to accompany his column. Merrill J. Mattes, *Indians, Infants, and Infantry: Andrew and Elizabeth Burt on the Frontier*, p. 223. The Crows left Gibbon on the same day the Shoshonis departed, citing as a reason their desire to provide for their families before the onset of winter. Gibbon, *Gibbon on the Sioux Campaign*, pp. 55–56.

25. *Milwaukee Sentinel*, September 18, 1876.

26. Harry H. Anderson, "The Battle of Slim Buttes," *Chicago Westerners' Brand Book* 22 (September, 1965):49.

27. Schuyler in Crook, *Autobiography*, p. 203; Clements, "Medical Report," p. 5; *Milwaukee Sentinel*, September 18, 1876.

28. *Milwaukee Sentinel*, September 18, 1876.

29. Anderson, "Battle of Slim Buttes," p. 49. Specifically, word had come that Indians had attacked both the small supply camp at the mouth of Glendive Creek and an army supply steamer on the river. "Crook's Report," September 25, 1876, p. 508.

30. "Sheridan's Report," November 25, 1876, p. 446; Mark H. Brown, *The Plainsmen of the Yellowstone: A History of the Yellowstone Basin*, p. 289; King, *Campaigning with Crook*, p. 90.

31. Knight, *Following the Indian Wars*, p. 266; Julia B. McGillycuddy, *McGillycuddy, Agent: A Biography of Dr. Valentine T. McGillycuddy*, pp. 52, 53.

Chapter 3

1. Finerty, *War-Path and Bivouac*, p. 175.

2. *Ibid.*, pp. 175–76. See also King, *Campaigning with Crook*, pp. 89–91.

3. Cynthia J. Capron, "The Indian Border War of 1876," *Journal of the Illinois State Historical Society* 13 (January, 1921):497.

4. *Ibid.*; Clements, "Medical Report," p. 8; Finerty, *War-Path and Bivouac*, pp. 175, 185; John G. Bourke, "Diary of Lieutenant John G. Bourke," 5 (1876):862–63, 866. Bourke described the preparation of cactus for consumption: "The spines are burnt off, the thick skin peeled and the inner meaty pulp fried." *Ibid.*, p. 871.

5. Bourke, "Diary," 5:866–67; Finerty, *War-Path and Bivouac*,

p. 176; King, *Campaigning with Crook*, p. 92; Capron, "Indian Border War," p. 497; "Crook's Report," September 25, 1876, p. 508; "Terry's Report," November 21, 1876, p. 468; Schuyler in Crook, *Autobiography*, p. 205; Clements, "Medical Report," p. 9; *New York Times*, September 28, 1876; Newspaper correspondent Robert B. Strahorn's account in Jesse Brown and A. M. Willard, *The Black Hills Trails*, p. 226.

6. Bourke, "Diary," 5:869, 870–71; DeBarthe, *Life and Adventures of Frank Grouard*, pp. 149–50; *New York Times*, September 28, 1876. There is some disagreement about the date of this exchange. Strahorn stated that it occurred September 3. Brown and Willard, *Black Hills Trails*, p. 226. But it happened after Crook had reached the Little Missouri and before he reached Heart River.

7. "Interview with Baptiste Pourier, 1907," Eli S. Ricker Collection, Nebraska State Historical Society, Lincoln, tablet 13, pp. 29–32.

8. *New-York Daily Herald*, September 18, 1876; Bourke, "Diary," 5:875–76; Strahorn in Brown and Willard, *Black Hills Trails*, p. 227. The Minneconjou leader Red Horse later referred to what probably was this event: "When the two commands [of Terry and Crook] divided we made a stand for one of them but for some reason they passed us and did not attack us." Red Horse's account of Slim Buttes, in Colonel W. H. Wood to Assistant Adjutant General, Department of Dakota, February 27, 1877. Sioux War Papers, National Archives Microfilm, AGO 1876. Hereafter cited as "Red Horse's Account."

9. Telegram, Crook to Sheridan, September 5, 1876, copy reproduced in Bourke, "Diary," 5:914.

10. *Ibid.*, pp. 915–16; Telegram, Sheridan to Sherman, September 8, 1876, in LR, Dakota Superintendency; *New York Times*, September 28, 1876; "Address by General Charles King, Given Before the Order of Indian Wars, Feb. 26, 1921," in Anson Mills, *My Story*, ed. C. H. Claudy, pp. 417–18. As early as July 8, in the wake of the Custer disaster, the *New York Times* suggested the need to defend the Black Hills.

11. Bourke, "Diary," 5:872–73; Capron, "Indian Border War," p. 497. Captain Andrew Burt of the Ninth Infantry, one of Crook's most ardent supporters, reported that the general was "opposed by nearly all of his rank officers" in his decision to march to the Black Hills. *Cincinnati* (Ohio) *Commercial*, September 17, 1876.

12. George F. Price, comp., *Across the Continent with the Fifth Cavalry*, p. 162; Bourke, "Diary," 5:873–74; Knight, *Following the Indian Wars*, p. 267; Anderson, "Battle of Slim Buttes," p. 50; Brown and Willard, *Black Hills Trails*, pp. 226–27; Schuyler in Crook, *Autobiography*, p. 205; King, *Campaigning with Crook*, p. 94.

13. Pp. 878–79.

14. See especially Annie D. Tallent, *The Black Hills; or, The Last Hunting Ground of the Dakotahs*, pp. 295–98, 313–14. Depredations were particularly frequent along the Black Hills stage route. Agnes Wright Spring, *The Cheyenne and Black Hills Stage and Express Routes*, pp. 156–57. See also *Daily Inter-Ocean*, September 2, 1876, which gives an account of many deaths during Indian raids in the Black Hills.

15. Finerty, *War-Path and Bivouac*, p. 182; DeBarthe, *Frank Grouard*, p. 151; King, "Re-Evaluation of General George Crook," p. 233. See also the role of the Indians in determing Crook's course, in Anderson, "Battle of Slim Buttes," p. 50. A critical view, albeit unacceptable according to the evidence, of Crook's decision to head for the Black Hills is presented in Charles E. DeLand, "The Sioux Wars," *South Dakota Historical Collections* 17 (1934):208.

16. Bourke, "Diary," 5: 873, 876.

17. *Cincinnati Commercial*, September 14, 1876.

18. Bourke, "Diary," 5: 878, 882; Clements, "Medical Report," p. 9.

19. "Interview with Baptiste Pourier."

20. *War-Path and Bivouac*, pp. 175, 184; Knight, *Following the Indian Wars*, p. 175.

21. *Cincinnati Commercial*, September 14, 1876.

22. Bourke, "Diary," 5:873; Finerty, *War-Path and Bivouac*, p. 185; Strahorn in Brown and Willard, *Black Hills Trails*, p. 232; George A. Forsyth, *The Story of the Soldier*, p. 334.

23. King in Mills, *My Story*, p. 417.

24. Bourke, "Diary," 5:880–81; Cyrus Townsend Brady, *Indian Fights and Fighters*, p. 306; "Interview with Donald Brown, Rushville, Nebraska," Ricker Collection, tablet 13, pp. 115–16. Hereafter cited as "Brown Interview."

25. "Diary," 5:881–82.

26. *Ibid.*, p. 877; Strahorn in Brown and Willard, *Black Hills Trails*, p. 229; DeBarthe, *Frank Grouard*, p. 152; *Ellis County Star*, October 12, 1876.

27. "Diary," 5:880.

28. "The Battle of Slim Buttes," *Journal of the United States Cavalry Association* 28 (January, 1918):400.

29. King in Mills, *My Story*, p. 418.

30. "Diary," 5:874–75.

31. McGillycuddy, *McGillycuddy, Agent*, pp. 54–55.

32. "Mills on Slim Buttes," January 24, 1914. Item 7a, Camp Papers in Ellison Collection.

33. McGillycuddy, *McGillycuddy, Agent*, p. 54; Finerty, *War-Path and Bivouac*, p. 184. Estimates of the number of riders unhorsed, and

thus of the number of mounts lost on the march, range from 150 to 250. *Ibid*.; Strahorn in Brown and Willard, *Black Hills Trails*, p. 229; "Battle of Slim Buttes" (*Cavalry Journal*), p. 400. Some of the cavalry companies reported the loss of horses in the field from exhaustion. Company D, Second Cavalry, abandoned 28 "public horses" during the march to the Black Hills, while Company A abandoned 18 of the animals. Company E, Third Cavalry, abandoned a total of 13 mounts "from utter exhaustion on line of march" between September 7 and 19. Muster Rolls, Second and Third Cavalry Regiments, August 31–October 31, 1876, Records of the Adjutant General's Office, Record Group 94, National Archives.

34. "Diary," 5:879. Clerical supplies grew low too, and Bourke reported that "the Adjutant General's department had shrunk down to one lead-pencil and a scratch-book, 6 × 3, of which only 20 or 30 pages were left." *Ibid*., p. 878.

35. *Ibid*., pp. 876–77; Charles King, "Memories of a Busy Life," *Wisconsin Magazine of History* 5 (March, 1922):242; Finerty, *War-Path and Bivouac*, p. 185; McGillycuddy, *McGillycuddy, Agent*, p. 55; Clements, "Medical Report," p. 10.

36. McGillycuddy, *McGillycuddy, Agent*, p. 55.

37. *Ellis County Star*, October 12, 1876.

38. *Ibid*.

39. David T. Mears, "Campaigning Against Crazy Horse," *Proceedings and Collections of the Nebraska State Historical Society* 15 (1907):73.

40. King, *War Eagle*, p. 176.

41. Bourke, "Diary," 5:882, 883, 884; Clements, "Medical Report," p. 9; Mills, *My Story*, pp. 165–66; *New York Times*, September 28, 1876; Strahorn in Brown and Willard, *Black Hills Trails*, p. 232; *Ellis County Star*, October 12, 1876; George S. Howard, "Extracts from a Diary," *Winners of the West* 14 (February, 1937):3; Myrle George Hanson, "A History of Harding County, South Dakota, to 1925," *South Dakota Historical Collections* 21 (1942):523; McGillycuddy, *McGillycuddy, Agent*, p. 54; King, *Campaigning with Crook*, pp. 93–94.

42. Agnes Wright Spring, ed., "Dr. McGillycuddy's Diary," *Denver Westerners' Brand Book, 1953*, p. 291.

43. "Diary," 5:884–85.

44. Crook to Sheridan, September 10, 1876, in *Report of the Secretary of War, 1876*, p. 506.

45. "Brown Interview."

46. Schuyler in Crook, *Autobiography*, p. 206.

47. Clements, "Medical Report," p. 10; Terry to Crook, September 4, 1876, transcribed in Bourke, "Diary," 5:890; Spring, "McGillycuddy's Diary," p. 291; "Journal of Big Horn and Yellowstone Expedition, 1876." Transcribed copy in the Research Files of Custer Battlefield National Monument, Crow Agency, Montana. This journal belonged to Private Richard Flynn of Company D, Fourth Infantry. The original is in the possession of the Flynn family, of Blair, Nebraska. Hereafter cited as Flynn, "Journal."

48. "Mills on Slim Buttes"; John A. Kirkwood to Walter M. Camp, October 9, 1919, item 98, Camp Papers in Ellison Collection.

49. Adjutant Bourke to Bubb, September 7, 1876. National Archives, Record Group 393, Department of Dakota, LS, p. 35.

50. Organization of the party is discussed in "Report of Captain Mills," September 9, 1876, in *Report of the Secretary of War, 1876*, p. 509, hereafter cited as "Mills's Report"; Bourke, *On the Border with Crook*, p. 368; Strahorn in Brown and Willard, *Black Hills Trails*, p. 229. For data on Mills see his autobiography, *My Story*, and W. W. Mills, *Forty Years at El Paso, 1858–1898*, ed. Rex W. Strickland, p. 185. Finerty, who apparently did not get on well with Mills, depicted him as "peculiar, and occasionally the reverse of politic, which to some extent neutralizes his undeniable ability as an officer." *War-Path and Bivouac*, p. 188. Mills's service record is capsulized in Francis B. Heitman, comp., *Historical Register and Dictionary of the United States Army, from its Organization, September 29, 1789, to March 2, 1903*, 1:713.

51. Schwatka died in 1892. His many publications included *Along Alaska's Great River*, *Nimrod of the North*, and *Children of the Cold*. *Harper's Encyclopaedia of United States History from 458 A.D. to 1902*, 8:94; Heitman, *Historical Register*, 1:867. A biographical sketch of Schwatka appears in *The Wi-iyohi: Monthly Bulletin of the South Dakota State Historical Society* 20 (September 1, 1966). For more on Crawford see Heitman, *Historical Register*, 1:336. A treatment of the minor diplomatic furor set off by Crawford's death appears in Jerome A. Greene, "The Crawford Affair: International Implications of the Geronimo Campaign," *Journal of the West* 11 (January, 1972):143–53. See Heitman, *Historical Register*, 1:989, 257–58, 297, for the respective service summaries of Von Luettwitz, Bubb, and Chase.

52. Bourke, "Diary," 5:888–89; Bourke, *On the Border with Crook*, p. 368; Anderson, "Battle of Slim Buttes," p. 51. In his memoirs Mills erroneously stated that no medical officer was sent with him. *My Story*, p. 166.

53. Mills, *My Story*, p. 166.

54. Interview with Brigadier General Bubb, November 19, 1915, in Walter Mason Camp Manuscripts, Field Notes, Brigham Young University Library, Provo, Utah. Hereafter cited as "Bubb Interview, 1915."

55. W. F. Beyer and O. F. Keydel, eds., *Deeds of Valor* 2:226; Knight, *Following the Indian Wars* p. 271; "Mills's Report," p. 509; Crook to Sheridan, September 10, 1876, in *Report of the Secretary of War, 1876*, p. 506; Bourke, "Diary," 5:889.

56. Howard, "Extracts from a Diary," p. 3.

57. "Red Horse's Account"; "Interview with Baptiste Pourier, 1907," Ricker Collection; Herbert S. Schell, *History of South Dakota*, p. 137; Hyde, *Red Cloud's Folk*, p. 275; Neihardt, *Black Elk Speaks*, p. 137. Stanley Vestal placed Sitting Bull and his Hunkpapa followers in the area of the Little Missouri near Crook's soldiers in September, 1876. *Sitting Bull*, p. 184. Vestal based this on information provided by Sioux informants. Their accounts are strongly substantiated by "Map—Showing Tral [*sic*] of Sitting Bull From Custer Battlefield till he reached Canada. As gathered from Sitting Bull at Ft Randall, D.T. Dec. 12, 1881." Record Group 94, Records of the Adjutant General's Office, 1780s–1917, National Archives. This map shows Sitting Bull's route into western Dakota following the Custer fight and before the Hunkpapa leader went into Canada.

58. Hyde, *Red Cloud's Folk*, p. 275; Neihardt, *Black Elk Speaks*, p. 137; Schell, *History of South Dakota*, p. 137.

59. The exact number of occupants, including warriors, of the Slim Buttes camp is a matter of conjecture. The scout Grouard estimated that the village contained 200 occupants. DeBarthe, *Frank Grouard*, p. 153. Likewise, Captain Mills learned from Indian captives that the village had contained "200 souls, 100 of whom were warriors." "Mills's Report," p. 510. If the camp, in fact, held around 200 people, it would seem that the figure of 100 warriors might be considered inordinately high. It is not easy to postulate precise population figures for Indian camps of the nineteenth century. One method, that used in 1855 by Thomas Twiss, Indian agent for the Cheyennes, Arapahoes, and Brulé and Oglala Sioux on the Upper Platte River, reckoned that each lodge contained 2 fighting men. By definition, "fighting men" included warriors (men from about 16 to 38 years old) and those boys and old men who were capable of wielding weapons. By Twiss's method of computation the Slim Buttes camp of thirty-seven lodges would have yielded 74 fighting men, a figure that does not seem excessive.

In pursuit of this complex demographic question historian Harry H. Anderson produced an impressive analytical study that tentatively advanced an average figure of 7 Indians per normal field-size tipi (approximately twelve feet in diameter), including 1.29 warriors. See his "Cheyennes at the Little Big Horn—A Study of Statistics," *North Dakota Historical Society Quarterly* 27 (Spring, 1960):3–15 (for a discussion of the dimensions of a typical Sioux [Lakota] hunting tipi, see Reginald and Gladys Laubin, *The Indian Tipi: Its History, Construction, and Use*, chapt. 3). If Anderson's reasoning is applied to the thirty-seven lodges known to have existed in the village at Slim Buttes, there were theoretically present 259 Indians—men, women, and children of all ages, including 47.7 warriors. When these figures are rounded off, it may be speculated that the camp consisted of approximately 260 tribesmen, only 50 of them of warrior age. In the defense of the village, however, the actual number of combatants (i.e., warriors, boys, and old men) could have indeed been around 100, as Mills stated.

60. Hyde, *Red Cloud's Folk*, p. 275; Sandoz, *Crazy Horse*, pp. 339–40; "Red Horse's Account"; Stanley Vestal, *Warpath and Council Fire: The Plains Indians' Struggle for Survival in War and in Diplomacy*, p. 251. See also "Blue Hair's Statement," in Walter Mason Camp Manuscripts, Field Notes, Brigham Young University Library.

61. Anderson, "Battle of Slim Buttes," p. 51; *The Wi-iyohi: Monthly Bulletin of the South Dakota State Historical Society* 2 (July 1, 1948); Hyde, *Red Cloud's Folk*, p. 318. At least one Sioux account maintained that the man called American Horse killed at Slim Buttes was not a chief and, moreover, was not even a Minneconjou but a Sans Arc. See "Interview with He Dog," in Walter M. Camp, *Custer in '76: Walter Camp's Notes on the Custer Fight*, ed. Kenneth Hammer, p. 208. The Oglala American Horse achieved some distinction while speaking during the council of the Black Hills Commission sent to treat with the Sioux for cession of the western third of the Great Sioux Reservation. *Chicago Times*, September 23, 1876. Charles Eastman, himself a Sioux, wrongly asserted that the Oglala American Horse took his uncle's name in 1876, after the Battle of Slim Buttes. *Indian Heroes and Great Chieftains*, pp. 165, 173. On September 2, 1876, however, fully one week before that battle, Colonel Mackenzie reported that the Oglala American Horse was involved in the killing of another Indian during a disturbance at Camp Robinson, Nebraska. Mackenzie to Assistant Adjutant General, Department of the Platte. Sioux War Papers, National Archives. See also "Interview with American Horse at J. H. Cook's." Ricker Collection, Survey Notes, tablet 16.

62. DeLand, "The Sioux Wars," p. 219. Bourke erroneously described the stream as "a confluent either of Grand River or Owl Creek." "Diary," 6 (1876):885.

63. The village site has changed but negligibly since 1876. Lieutenant King, whose contemporary description of the ground compares very favorably with its present appearance, wrote that "the tepees are nestled about in three shallow ravines or 'cooleys,' . . . which, uniting in the centre of the mètropolis, form a little valley through which their joint contributions trickle away in a muddy streamlet." *Campaigning with Crook*, pp. 116–17.

64. Walter M. Camp, "Discovery of the Lost Site of the Slim Buttes Battle," *South Dakota Historical Collections* 9 (1918):68. The village stood about twenty miles east of the modern community of Buffalo, South Dakota, and barely two miles west of the Reva post office.

65. "Mills on Slim Buttes"; Mills, *My Story*, p. 166; Knight, *Following the Indian Wars*, p. 272; Joseph Mills Hanson, *The Conquest of the Missouri: Being the Story of the Life and Exploits of Captain Grant Marsh*, p. 523; DeBarthe, *Frank Grouard*, p. 152.

66. Mills, *My Story*, p. 166; DeBarthe, *Frank Grouard*, pp. 152–53; Strahorn in Brown and Willard, *Black Hills Trails*, p. 233. According to Lieutenant Schwatka, "Gruard [*sic*] believed it to be the village of Roman Nose, a Brule Sioux, that had left Spotted Tail Agency . . . [to join] Sitting Bull and Crazy Horse." *Daily Inter-Ocean*, October 4, 1876.

67. Mills's command evidently camped along a watery draw near the site of the present George Lermeny homestead. The troops would thus have been east and south of the Slim Buttes range and slightly northeast of the hostile camp.

68. "Mills's Report," p. 509; "Mills on Slim Buttes"; "Bubb Interview, 1915"; Knight, *Following the Indian Wars*, p. 272; *Chicago Tribune*, September 17, 1876.

69. "Mills on Slim Buttes."

70. *Ibid.*;

71. *Ibid.*; "Battle of Slim Buttes" (*Cavalry Journal*), p. 401; *Belle Fourche* (South Dakota) *Bee*, July 5, 1917; DeBarthe, *Frank Grouard*, p. 153.

72. "Mills on Slim Buttes."

73. Grouard stated that he learned the size of the village. It seems natural to conclude that he would have relayed the information to Mills if he had. *Buffalo* (South Dakota) *Times-Herald*, November 14, 1924.

74. "Bubb Interview, 1915"; Brigadier General John W. Bubb to Walter M. Camp, September 17, 1917. Item 90, Camp Papers in Ellison Collection. See also Bubb to Camp, December 13, 1917. *Ibid.*, item 92.

75. "Mills's Report," p. 509; Strahorn in Brown and Willard, *Black Hills Trails*, p. 233; Mills, *My Story*, p. 166.

76. "Mills on Slim Buttes."

77. *Chicago Tribune*, September 17, 1876.

78. Quoted in Knight, *Following the Indian Wars*, p. 272.

79. Mills, *My Story*, p. 166.

80. "Bubb Interview, 1915."

81. *Belle Fourche Bee*, July 5, 1917; "Battle of Slim Buttes" (*Cavalry Journal*), p. 402.

82. See Russell F. Weigley, *The American Way of War: A History of United States Military Strategy and Policy*, p. 153; *American Military History, 1607–1958*, p. 280.

83. Robert M. Utley, *Frontier Regulars: The United States Army and the Indian, 1866–1890*, pp. 50, 51. A conjectural example of the surprise tactic as used against Indians appears in Don Rickey, Jr., *War in the West: The Indian Campaigns*, pp. 25–32. There existed no official edicts governing warfare with Indians. Neither the military manuals nor the professional journals published for the edification of officers imparted relevant information regarding the deployment of troops in Indian combat. West Point textbooks offered nothing beyond conventional battle procedures. Robert M. Utley, *Frontiersmen in Blue: The United States Army and the Indian, 1848–1865*, p. 57. During the mid-1870s Commanding General Sherman sent Major General Emory Upton to India to observe the operations of the British army in that land. Sherman hoped to apply the knowledge Upton gained to the Indian campaigns then under way in the western United States, but the plan never materialized. Russell F. Weigley, *History of the United States Army*, p. 276.

84. Schwatka, in *Daily Inter-Ocean*, October 4, 1876.

Chapter 4

1. "Bubb Interview, 1915"; Schwatka, in *Daily Inter-Ocean*, October 4, 1876.

2. John A. Kirkwood to Camp, October 9, 1919. Item 98, Camp Papers in Ellison Collection. For Mills's preparations for the assault see "Mills's Report," p. 510; Mills, *My Story*, pp. 166–67; *New-York Daily Tribune*, September 18, 1876; *Daily Rocky Mountain*, September 17, 1876; *Chicago Tribune*, September 17, 1876.

3. *New-York Daily Tribune*, September 18, 1876.

4. Bourke later recorded that the pony herd had numbered over 400 animals, but that "not quite . . . two hundred fell into our hands." "Diary," 6:871.

5. Harry W. Spooner [H. W. Jefferson] to Lester Wallace, October 13, 1886. Published in *Journal of the United States Cavalry Association* 20 (1909–10):1235.

6. Wrote Captain Andrew Burt, who was not present with Mills's

command: "By some official miscalculation the charge was ordered too early to be as effective as it might have been could the men have seen clearly enough to fire with any degree of accuracy." "Account of Slim Buttes." Schwatka explained the disruption of the plan in this way: "The column [proceeded] in three lines, as explained, and after several small mistakes as to the probable place of the village, our guide, Frank Gruard [*sic*], brought in a herd of about six or eight Indian ponies that he had quietly 'gobbled' from the outlying herd of the village, without creating any disturbance whatever. Several such small captures were repeated, the column meantime advancing, when the remainder of the herd, alarmed at its approach, stampeded toward the village, now only a few yards distant." *Daily Inter-Ocean*, October 4, 1876.

7. "Mills on Slim Buttes."

8. This reconstruction of Mills's attack is based upon lengthy investigations of the terrain at Slim Buttes, coupled with material and reminiscences contained in the *Belle Fourche Bee*, July 5, 1917; DeBarthe, *Frank Grouard*, p. 154; "Mills's Report," p. 510; "Battle of Slim Buttes" (*Cavalry Journal*), p. 402; *Chicago Tribune*, September 17, 1876; and Knight, *Following the Indian Wars*, p. 274.

9. *Chicago Tribune*, September 17, 1876; Kirkwood to Camp, October 9, 1919; "Mills's Report," p. 510; "Mills on Slim Buttes"; Burt, "Account of Slim Buttes"; Mills, *My Story*, p. 167; Finerty, *War-Path and Bivouac*, p. 187. Frank Grouard later described confusion and disagreement on the part of Mills and his officers at the failure to carry the village with complete surprise: "I saw there had been a mistake made and the Indians were firing back and the fight was general. Capt. Mills had given the order to retreat, and [Lieutenant] Crawford had told him that it was impossible [now] to retreat." DeBarthe, *Frank Grouard*, p. 154. On the other hand, Mills later wrote that "while the fighting was going on Grouard cleared out and I did not see anything of him. He had very little physical courage on such occasions." "Mills on Slim Buttes." It is obvious that there was no love lost between Mills and Grouard. Private Duren's wounding was reported by Rus Wilson, a civilian with Mills. Hanson, "History of Harding County," p. 524. The injury was so superficial it was not listed on formal reports.

10. *Daily Inter-Ocean*, October 4, 1876.

11. "Mills's Report," p. 510; "Mills on Slim Buttes"; Bourke, *On the Border with Crook*, p. 370; Helen R. Keirnes, "Final Days of the Indian Campaign of 1876–1877: Aftermath of the Little Big Horn" (M.A. thesis, University of South Dakota, 1969), p. 80. Red Horse described the attack: "It was early in the morning still dark and misting. We were all asleep. The first we knew we were fired upon, we caught up what arms

we could find in the dark, the women taking the children and hiding among the rocks. We gathered up a few horses and put our families on them and went to the main camp." "Red Horse's Account."

12. "Mills on Slim Buttes."

13. Strahorn in Brown and Willard, *Black Hills Trails*, pp. 230, 233; Muster Roll, Company C, Third Cavalry, August 31–October 31, 1876. Records of the Adjutant General's Office, Record Group 94, National Archives. *Brownsville* (Texas) *Herald*, March 26, 1931. McClinton posthumously received the Silver Star for his service at Slim Buttes. General Orders no. 2, War Department, January 28, 1931, Section 11, p. 10. This incident is mentioned in DeBarthe, *Frank Grouard*, p. 155. The history of the so-called Mills Guidon is interesting. Years later Mills encased it in glass and affixed the following statement: "This guidon belonged to Company 'I' 7th Cavalry (Captain [Myles W.] Keogh), was lost with Custer at the Battle of the Little Big Horn, June 25th 1876, and was recaptured by my command at the Battle of Slim Buttes, September 9, 1876, then in good condition, folded up in an Indian reticule with a pair of Colonel Keogh's gauntlets marked with his name. It was loaned for several years by me with other trophies to the Museum of the Military Service Institution on Governor's Island, and from want of proper care returned so ravaged by moths that this is the most that could be made of it." The framed guidon, in decrepit condition, was donated by the Mills family to Custer Battlefield National Monument, where it reposes today.

14. Mills's Report, p. 510; Mills, *My Story*, p. 167; Strahorn in Brown and Willard, *Black Hills Trails*, p. 233; Anderson, "Battle of Slim Buttes," p. 51; Keirnes, "Final Days," p. 81. The packers had been instructed to fend for themselves if the village proved too strong and the warriors overran Mills's soldiers. Knight, *Following the Indian Wars*, p. 274.

15. "Mills on Slim Buttes"; "Bubb Interview, 1915"; Bubb to Camp, September 17, 1917. Finerty identified the packer as George Herman. *War-Path and Bivouac*, p. 186.

16. Kirkwood to Camp, October 9, 1919.

17. Bubb to Camp, September 17, 1917.

18. September 17, 1876.

19. Bubb had several spades with which to prepare the entrenchments. Their precise location has not been established, though forty-one years after the event Bubb described them as merely "Buffalo wallows (3 or 4) reamed out a little more, on the ridge running parallel with the dry creek in which the Indian tepes [*sic*] were pitched." Bubb to Camp, September 17, 1917. See also "Bubb Interview, 1915." In 1914 Mills recalled that "we were on a slope that faced the slope that the village was

on, with a sort of coulee or depression between these two slopes, and to make my position secure I dug intrenchments on the top of the hill just back of where we were lying." "Mills on Slim Buttes." See also "Mills's Report," p. 510, and Finerty, *War-Path and Bivouac*, p. 189. First Sergeant H. W. Jefferson of Company E, Fifth Cavalry, recalled that "our men . . . dug small rifle pits on the brow of a hill overlooking camp." Spooner [Jefferson] to Wallace, October 13, 1886, p. 1235. Schwatka stated that Mills took possession of "a large hill west of this place, and overlooking it [the village]." *Daily Inter-Ocean*, October 4, 1876.

20. Burt, "Account of Slim Buttes."

21. "Mills on Slim Buttes."

22. Kirkwood to Camp, October 9, 1919.

23. *Ibid*. See also *New York Times*, September 28, 1876; "Mills's Report," p. 510; Finerty, *War-Path and Bivouac*, p. 192; Hanson, *Conquest of the Missouri*, p. 524.

24. Mills maintained that he sent "three couriers at intervals," and evidently at least one apprised Crook of Mills's casualties, including the one dead. See Mills, *My Story*, p. 167, and Bourke, *On the Border with Crook*, p. 370.

25. Stated Bubb: "I do not think Crook had any special information which caused him to follow us the next day [September 8, rather than 9]. Being an experienced Indian fighter he governed himself by the character of the country . . . & Indian signs in that part of the country. . . . He agreed to follow our trail as he had given us his best guide—Grouard." Bubb to Camp, December 13, 1917. Mention of "recent Indian camp signs" is in Spring, "Dr. McGillycuddy's Diary," p. 292.

26. Bourke, "Diary," 5:885.

27. *Ibid*., pp. 885–87; McGillycuddy, *McGillycuddy, Agent*, pp. 55–56.

28. Schuyler in Crook, *Autobiography*, p. 206.

29. Flynn, "Journal," p. 64.

30. *Ibid*.; *Ellis County Star*, October 12, 1876.

31. "Diary," 6:866.

32. *Ibid*., 5:889; Clements, "Medical Report," p. 10.

33. *On the Border with Crook*, p. 368. See also, Bourke, "Diary," 5:889, 890.

34. King, *War Eagle*, p. 177; Bourke, "Diary," 5:890; Flynn, "Journal," p. 63. On the other hand, Bourke wrote that "criticism was silenced in the presence of a General who could reduce himself to the level of the most lowly and even tho' dissatisfaction and grumbling found their out . . . the thinking and observing in the command reflected that

their sufferings were fully shared by their leader and [the men] honored him accordingly." "Diary," 6:865.

35. Flynn, "Journal," p. 63.

36. Carr to wife, September 10, 1876. E. A. Carr Papers, U.S. Army Military History Institute, Army War College, Carlisle Barracks, Pa. Ironically, on the day of the Slim Buttes engagement the officer in charge of the Cheyenne River Agency, on the east along the Missouri River, wired his superiors in Saint Paul: "Have had messengers yesterday and to-day direct from hostile camp. Report camp near Slim Buttes, one hundred eighty miles distant." Telegram, Lieutenant Colonel Buell to Assistant Adjutant General, Department of Dakota, September 9, 1876. Sioux War Papers, National Archives Microfilm.

37. *Cincinnati Commercial*, September 17, 1876.

38. Flynn, "Journal," p. 64; Bourke, *On the Border with Crook*, pp. 369, 370; Capron, "Indian Border War of 1876," p. 498; Finerty, *War-Path and Bivouac*, p. 186; Bourke, "Diary," 6:868. King said that the first courier arrived "just as we were breaking up our cheerless bivouac of the night." *Campaigning with Crook*, p. 97.

39. Lieutenant King, regimental adjutant of the Fifth Cavalry, recounted the following incident: "Many a man ordered to rein out [of formation because of a poor mount] showed reluctance, even resentment. [Lieutenant] Bob London, riding a wretched wreck of a steed was one of them. He was our lightest weight . . . but that horse couldn't have borne him five miles at a walk. . . . Over the next rider and horse I hesitated, and finally passed [approved] them, but said the rider: 'I can't make this horse carry me any ten miles.' London spoke up at the instant: 'I can ride that horse; he'll carry my weight every inch of the way.'" King in Mills, *My Story*, p. 419.

40. Bourke, "Diary," 6:868–69; Bourke, *On the Border with Crook*, p. 370; "Report of Lieut. Col. E. A. Carr," September 15, 1876, in *Report of the Secretary of War, 1876*, p. 511, hereafter cited as "Carr's Report"; Clements, "Medical Report," p. 11; King, *War Eagle*, p. 177; Spring, "Dr. McGillycuddy's Diary," p. 292; Finerty, *War-Path and Bivouac*, p. 186; *Ellis County Star*, October 12, 1876.

41. Finerty, *War-Path and Bivouac*, p. 186.

42. Bourke, "Diary," 6:869–70.

43. *Ibid*., 6:870.

44. *Daily Rocky Mountain*, September 17, 1876.

45. September 18, 1876. Further indication of Crook's displeasure is contained in a letter, Anonymous to E. A. Brininstool, postmarked June 1935, at Columbus, Ohio. Purportedly written by a deserter from

Crook's army soon after the Slim Buttes battle, the letter is item 316 in the Fred Dustin Collection, Custer Battlefield National Monument, Crow Agency, Montana.

46. Bubb to Camp, September 17, 1917; "Battle of Slim Buttes" (*Cavalry Journal*), p. 403. The method used to signal the approach is not known. Probably the men fired their carbines in the air.

47. "Carr's Report," pp. 511, 512; Mills, *My Story*, p. 167; DeBarthe, *Frank Grouard*, p. 156; Vestal, *Sitting Bull*, p. 186; *New-York Daily Herald*, September 18, 1876; King in Mills, *My Story*, p. 420.

48. *New York Times*, September 28, 1876.

49. Carr to wife, September 10, 1876; King, *Campaigning with Crook*, pp. 107, 117, 118; King in Mills, *My Story*, p. 420; "Mills on Slim Buttes"; Schuyler in Crook, *Autobiography*, p. 207.

50. Bourke, *On the Border*, pp. 370, 371; Bourke, "Diary," 6:872. Charles DeLand stated that the village actually consisted of two camps—one main concentration of tipis and a "lesser" village of seven lodges detached nearby. "The Sioux Wars," p. 223. I have been unable to find any documentation to support DeLand's assertion.

51. Bourke, "Diary," 6:870–71, 878–79; "Mills's Report," p. 510; Howard, "Extracts from a Diary," p. 3; *New York Times*, September 28, 1876; Bourke, *On the Border*, p. 370; DeBarthe, *Frank Grouard*, p. 155; Strahorn in Brown and Willard, *Black Hills Trails*, pp. 230–31, 234; *New-York Daily Herald*, September 18, 1876.

52. Carr to wife, September 10, 1876.

53. *Cincinnati Commercial*, September 17, 1876. Among the souvenirs personally collected by Mills were: 1 catlinite pipe bowl, 2 pairs beaded hair ties, 2 women's beaded pouches, 1 pair buckskin leggings, 2 beaded blanket ornaments, 2 Cheyenne rattles, 2 pairs beaded gaiters, and a piece of unfinished beadwork. He also kept a horned headdress. Inventory of General Anson Mills Collection, in the Accession Records, Custer Battlefield National Monument; Mabel Overton Cotter to Edward S. Luce, June 22, 1951, in *ibid*. These objects were all retained by the Mills family.

54. DeBarthe, *Frank Grouard*, p. 155.

55. Mills, *My Story*, pp. 167–68; Bourke, "Diary," 6:878.

56. This list of army items captured at Slim Buttes is compiled from information contained in Bourke, "Diary," 6:871–72; Bourke, *On the Border*, p. 371; Finerty, *War-Path and Bivouac*, p. 188; McGillycuddy, *McGillycuddy, Agent*, p. 57; Telegram, Crook to Sheridan, September 15, 1876, in LR, Dakota Superintendency; "Mills's Report," p. 510; Price, *Across the Continent*, p. 164; Strahorn in Brown and Willard, *Black Hills Trails*, p. 231; Hanson, *Conquest of the Missouri*, p. 525;

and DeBarthe, *Frank Grouard*, p. 155. Grouard stated that someone found $11,000, supposedly stripped from Custer's dead (*ibid*.), a figure that seems most excessive. A conservative estimate of the cash recovered placed it at $900. *Chicago Tribune*, September 19, 1876. See also Brady, *Indian Fights and Fighters*, p. 311; and J. W. Vaughn, *Indian Fights: New Facts on Seven Encounters*, p. 185. A cavalry sergeant remembered finding in the village a locket, a picture of Captain Keogh, two gold-mounted ivory-handled revolvers, and a Spencer sporting rifle. "The picture and locket I gave to an officer of the 3rd Cav., who claimed them as a relative of the officer killed with Custer, and a revolver I gave to Capt. Rodgers of "A" Co. 5th Cav. The rifle I sold some days later for two loaves of bread." Spooner [Jefferson] to Wallace, October 13, 1886, p. 1235.

57. *New-York Daily Tribune*, September 18, 1876.

58. *Ibid*.

59. Sandoz, *Crazy Horse*, p. 341.

60. See "Red Horse's Account"; see also "Interview with He Dog" and "Interview with Tall Bull," in Camp, *Custer in '76*, pp. 208, 213.

61. Bourke, "Diary," 6:872–74; DeBarthe, *Frank Grouard*, p. 156; Finerty, *War-Path and Bivouac*, p. 188; Flynn, "Journal," p. 65; Vestal, *Sitting Bull*, p. 186; King, *War Eagle*, p. 178; King, *Campaigning with Crook*, p. 108.

62. *Chicago Tribune*, September 20, 1876.

63. "Diary," 6:874. "Buffalo Chips . . . was a fine looking young man, and was about 24 or 25 years of age, with long light hair flowing down over his shoulders." Letter, William E. Helvie, Company F, Fourth Infantry, in *Winners of the West*, 5 (March 30, 1928).

64. "Interview with Baptiste Pourier, 1907." Other descriptions of White's death are in Finerty, *War-Path and Bivouac*, pp. 192–93; De-Barthe, *Frank Grouard*, p. 157; Bourke, *On the Border with Crook*, p. 372. Sergeant John Kirkwood maintained that White was hit in the forehead the same way Wenzel was hit. Kirkwood to Camp, October 9, 1919. Captain Burt stated that one of the scouts with White when he died was Jack Crawford and gave this account of the incident: "White . . . saw a dog moving near the ravine and thinking it an Indian was about to rise to fire at it when prevented by Jack who told him what it was. White persisted in the belief that an Indian was where he had seen the movement and raised himself again to endeavor to get a shot. Jack reached to pull him back from exposure but too late, for he was instantly killed by a shot from the ravine." "Account of Slim Buttes."

65. Bourke, "Diary," 6:874–75; Finerty, *War-Path and Bivouac*, pp. 189, 342.

66. This incident is mentioned in Finerty, *War-Path and Bivouac*, p. 189; DeBarthe, *Frank Grouard*, p. 157; *New York Times*, September 28, 1876; *Chicago Tribune*, September 20, 1876; and "Interview with Donald Brown." Strangely, Pourier did not discuss it in his interview with Ricker in 1907. A slightly different version was given in Burt, "Account of Slim Buttes."

67. Bourke, "Diary," 6:873; King in Mills, *My Story*, p. 420; Bourke, *On the Border with Crook*, p. 371; King, *Campaigning with Crook*, p. 108; McGillycuddy, *McGillycuddy, Agent*, p. 58; Spooner [Jefferson] to Wallace, October 13, 1886, p. 1235.

68. *On the Border with Crook*, p. 371.

69. Finerty, *War-Path and Bivouac*, p. 192; Bourke, "Diary," 6:875.

70. Bourke, "Diary," 6:873.

71. *Cincinnati Commercial*, September 17, 1876; *Chicago Tribune*, September 20, 1876; Finerty, *War-Path and Bivouac*, p. 190; Bourke, *On the Border with Crook*, p. 371.

72. "Interview with Baptiste Pourier, 1907"; "Mills on Slim Buttes"; *Chicago Tribune*, September 20, 1876; "Interview with Donald Brown"; *New York Times*, September 28, 1876.

73. "Mills on Slim Buttes"; Finerty, *War-Path and Bivouac*, p. 190; *New-York Daily Herald*, September 18, 1876; King in Mills, *My Story*, p. 420; Bourke, *On the Border with Crook*, p. 372. Bourke noted in his diary (6:873) that "the Indians declined to accede to any terms and seemed determined to fight it out to the last." Unlike Finerty he did not mention the surrender of women and children at this point.

74. *Campaigning with Crook*, p. 112.

75. See Clements, "Medical Report," p. 11; Finerty, *War-Path and Bivouac*, pp. 189–90; DeBarthe, *Frank Grouard*, p. 157; McGillycuddy, *McGillycuddy, Agent*, pp. 57–58; *New York Times*, September 28, 1876; "Battle of Slim Buttes" (*Cavalry Journal*), p. 404.

76. *New York Times*, September 28, 1876; DeBarthe, *Frank Grouard*, p. 157. Reporter Strahorn stated that Pourier seized this opportunity to shoot American Horse, who was holed up in the ravine with the other warriors. Brown and Willard, *Black Hills Trails*, p. 234.

77. Bourke, *On the Border with Crook*, pp. 372–73; This warrior was Charging Bear, who later served as a corporal in Crook's company of Indian scouts. Bourke, "Diary," 6:877–78.

78. "Mills on Slim Buttes"; "Interview with Baptiste Pourier, 1907"; Kirkwood to Camp, October 9, 1919. Pourier later recalled that he found American Horse kneeling with gun in hand in a hole in the side of the ravine that "he had scooped out with a butcher knife." "Interview with Baptiste Pourier, 1907." First Sergeant Jefferson of Company E, Fifth

Cavalry, maintained that he shot American Horse as the Indian drew a revolver and tried to shoot Crook. Spooner [Jefferson] to Wallace, October 13, 1886, p. 1235. See also "Memoirs of James Benton Glover" p. 20, typescript, Glover Collection, Arizona Historical Society. Glover was a civilian packer with Crook who witnessed American Horse's surrender. The scout Jack Crawford obtained American Horse's rifle, a Spencer repeater, along with a Colt revolver used in the Slim Buttes fight. They were included in a list of items lent by Mrs. Willis B. Shontz for the centennial observance of Fort Bliss, Texas, in November, 1948.

79. *Chicago Tribune*, September 17, 1876.

80. Carr to wife, September 10, 1876; Bourke, "Diary," 6:877–78; Bourke, *On the Border with Crook*, p. 373; Finerty, *War-Path and Bivouac*, pp. 190–91; *Ellis County Star*, October 12, 1876.

81. *New York Times*, September 28, 1876.

82. *Ibid*. Finerty wrote that "the skull of one poor squaw was blown, literally, to atoms, revealing the ridge of the palate and presenting a most ghastly and revolting spectacle. Another of the dead females . . . was so riddled with bullets that there appeared to be no unwounded part of her person left." *War-Path and Bivouac*, p. 191.

83. Finerty, *War-Path and Bivouac*, pp. 191–92; *New York Times*, September 28, 1876. Ute John was also known as Captain Jack. His Ute name was Nicaagat. Robert Emmitt, *The Last War Trail: The Utes and the Settlement of Colorado*, pp. 96, 197.

84, "Diary," 6:878; *Chicago Tribune*, September 17, 1876.

85. "Mills on Slim Buttes."

86. Clements, "Medical Report," p. 12; Spring, "Dr. McGillycuddy's Diary," p. 292; Mills, *My Story*, p. 168; Finerty, *War-Path and Bivouac*, p. 191; Bourke, *On the Border with Crook*, p. 373; King, *War Eagle*, p. 178; McGillycuddy, *McGillycuddy, Agent*, p. 58; Carr to wife, September 10, 1876; Notes by Anson Mills, January 21, 1898, in the Anson Mills Collection, Western History Research Center, University of Wyoming Library, Laramie; *Daily Inter-Ocean*, October 4, 1876.

87. "Mills on Slim Buttes"; King, *Campaigning with Crook*, p. 116; Mills, *My Story*, p. 510; Price, *Across the Continent*, p. 163.

88. *New York Times*, September 28, 1876; Bourke, *On the Border with Crook*, p. 374; Finerty, *War-Path and Bivouac*, p. 194; King, *Campaigning with Crook*, pp. 116–18; Spring, "Dr. McGillycuddy's Diary," p. 292; Anderson, "Battle of Slim Buttes," p. 55; King, *War Eagle*, p. 179; Carr to wife, September 10, 1876.

89. King, *Campaigning with Crook*, p. 118; Finerty, *War-Path and Bivouac*, p. 197; "Battle of Slim Buttes" (*Cavalry Journal*), p. 403; Sandoz, *Crazy Horse*, p. 340.

170   SLIM BUTTES, 1876

90. Carr to wife, September 10, 1876; Bourke, "Diary," 6:881, 882, 883; King, *Campaigning with Crook*, pp. 118, 119; Finerty, *War-Path and Bivouac*, p. 194; King in Mills, *My Story*, p. 422; "Carr's Report," p. 511; *New-York Daily Herald*, September 18, 1876.

91. "Report of Capt. William H. Powell, Co. G, 4th Infantry, to Adjutant, Infantry Battalion, September 15, 1876." National Archives, Record Group 393, Department of the Platte, LR.

92. *New-York Daily Herald*, September 18, 1876.

93. See reports of Captain Thomas F. Tobey, Lieutenant Frank Taylor, and Captain James Kennington, September 15, 1876, National Archives, Record Group 393, Department of the Platte, LR.

94. "Report of Major Alexander Chambers," in *Report of the Secretary of War, 1876*, p. 513; "Battle of Slim Buttes" (*Cavalry Journal*), p. 403; Finerty, *War-Path and Bivouac*, p. 195.

95. *Chicago Tribune*, September 17, 1876.

96. "Report of Captain Gerhard L. Luhn, September 15, 1876," National Archives, Record Group 393, Department of the Platte, LR. See also "Report of Captain Daniel W. Burke, September 15, 1876"; "Report of Second Lieutenant Charles M. Rockefeller, September 15, 1876"; "Report of First Lieutenant Henry Seton"; and "Report of Captain A. S. Burt, September 15, 1876," *ibid.*

97. King, *Campaigning with Crook*, pp. 119, 120–21, 122; Finerty, *War-Path and Bivouac*, pp. 195, 196; Bourke, *On the Border with Crook*, p. 374; Price, *Across the Continent*, p. 163.

98. *Chicago Tribune*, September 17, 1876.

99. *Chicago Times*, September 17, 1876.

100. Carr to wife, September 10, 1876.

101. "Carr's Report," p. 512. On the question of casualties on both sides, including the skirmishing on September 10, see Mills's Report, p. 510; "Carr's Report," p. 512; Clements, "Medical Report," p. 13; Bourke, "Diary," 6:882; McGillycuddy, *McGillycuddy, Agent*, p. 59. On the basis of knowledge gained from Sioux participants and their relatives, Stanley Vestal ascertained that total Indian losses at Slim Buttes numbered ten killed and two wounded. *New Sources of Indian History*, p. 136. Red Horse claimed that Indian losses numbered 7 killed and 4 wounded. "Red Horse's Account." Another Indian account of the fights placed the Sioux dead at 3 men, 4 women, and 1 infant. See DeLand, "The Sioux Wars," p. 281. John F. Finerty claimed that the soldiers marveled at their own light casualties in the afternoon encounter, ascribing the fact to the poor marksmanship of the mounted hostiles, who spoiled their accuracy by firing at targets positioned lower than themselves.

Conversely, the inclined nature of the terrain supposedly worked to the advantage of the soldiers. *War-Path and Bivouac,* p. 196. Finerty also gives a higher casualty figure for the soldiers (24+ wounded, mainly cavalry) but does not differentiate among the several actions on September 9 and 10. *Ibid.,* pp. 342–43. Civilian casualties in the engagements evidently went unrecorded, but one of the packers wounded was James B. Glover, who was hit by a bullet below the knee. "Memoirs," p. 20. Official and unofficial army casualty accountings for Slim Buttes appear in Appendix B.

102. Again, these figures applied to the total casualties from the various Slim Buttes encounters. *Chicago Tribune,* September 19, 1876. Walter Camp's Sioux informant Blue Hair accounted for five of the Indian dead on the field—four of whom belonged to one Minneconjou family, Otter Man, his wife, daughter, and granddaughter. One wounded man escaped and later died among his people. "Blue Hair's Statement." Camp Manuscripts.

103. King, *Campaigning with Crook,* p. 122; "The Slim Buttes Battlefield," *South Dakota Historical Collection* 9 (1918):53.

104. *War-Path and Bivouac,* p. 203.

105. "Memories of a Busy Life," p. 243.

106. "Campaigning Against Crazy Horse," p. 73. See also Schuyler in Crook, *Autobiography,* p. 206.

107. *Chicago Tribune,* September 17, 1876.

108. *Ibid.;* Bourke, *On the Border with Crook,* pp. 373, 375.

109. *Chicago Tribune,* September 17, 1876; Bourke, "Diary," 6:883, 885; Flynn, "Journal," p. 66; Howard, "Extracts from a Diary," p. 3; "Report of Major Chambers," p. 513; "Report of Captain William H. Powell, September 15, 1876."

110. Finerty, *War-Path and Bivouac,* pp. 197, 198; Clements, "Medical Report," p. 13; McGillycuddy, *McGillycuddy, Agent,* p. 59. One account stated that American Horse lingered until 6:00 A.M. and that he confirmed that the tribes were scattering and were becoming tired and discouraged by the war. "He appeared satisfied that the lives of his squaws and children were spared." *Chicago Times,* September 17, 1876.

111. Kirkwood to Camp, October 9, 1919; Finerty, *War-Path and Bivouac,* pp. 193, 198; King, *Campaigning with Crook,* p. 109; McGillycuddy, *McGillycuddy, Agent,* p. 59; Anderson, "Battle of Slim Buttes," p. 56; *Buffalo Times-Herald,* November 14, 1924. Bourke stated that American Horse was "buried at sun-rise." "Diary," 6:885.

112. Bourke, "Diary," 6:883–885; Finerty, *War-Path and Bivouac,* p. 202; "Carr's Report," p. 512; *Buffalo Times-Herald,* November 14,

1924; Camp, "Discovery of the Lost Site," p. 62; Bourke, *On the Border with Crook*, p. 375. Two men and nine women chose to leave the command. *Daily Inter-Ocean*, September 19, 1876.

113. Anonymous to E. A. Brininstool, June 1935. That the remaining Indian prisoners were not harmed is evident in a photograph taken by Stanley Morrow after the column reached the Black Hills. Reference to the prisoners by a civilian contemporary is in Richard B. Hughes, *Pioneer Days in the Black Hills*, ed. Agnes Wright Spring, p. 190.

114. Kirkwood to Camp, October 9, 1919. Dr. McGillycuddy was placed in charge of transporting the wounded after the Slim Buttes encounter. "I employed nine travois and three two-horse litters," he reported, "and carried the wounded a distance of about eighty miles, from the field to the northern portion of the Black Hills." War Department, Surgeon General's Office. George A. Otis, "A Report to the Surgeon General of the Transport of Sick and Wounded by Pack Animals," pp. 25–26.

115. "Carr's Report," pp. 511–12; Finerty, *War-Path and Bivouac*, p. 198; "Report of Major Chambers," p. 513.

116. Carr to wife, September 10, 1876; *New-York Daily Herald*, September 18, 1876; *Daily Inter-Ocean*, October 4, 1876; King, *Campaigning with Crook*, pp. 98, 100, 102; "Carr's Report," p. 512; Bourke, "Diary," 6:886; King in Mills, *My Story*, p. 422.

117. *Cincinnati Commercial*, September 17, 1876.

Chapter 5

1. Spring, "Dr. McGillycuddy's Diary," p. 292; Flynn, "Journal," p. 66; King, *Campaigning with Crook*, p. 126; Carr to wife, September 10, 1876; Paul L. Hedren, "Captain Charles King at Sunset Pass," *Journal of Arizona History* 17 (Autumn, 1976): 253–64.

2. Crook to Sheridan, September 10, 1876, in *Report of the Secretary of War, 1876*, pp. 506, 507.

3. Adjutant Bourke to Grouard, September 10, 1876. National Archives, Record Group 393, Department of Dakota, LS, p. 35.

4. Bubb to Camp, December 13, 1917; *New-York Daily Herald*, September 18, 1876; "Battle of Slim Buttes by Gen. G. F. Chase," item 7, Camp Papers in Ellison Collection; Bourke, "Diary," 6:891; Finerty, *War-Path and Bivouac*, pp. 200–201; DeBarthe, *Frank Grouard*, p. 159.

5. "Battle of Slim Buttes by Gen. G. F. Chase."

6. *Ibid*.

7. Bubb to Camp, December 13, 1917; "Battle of Slim Buttes by Gen. G. F. Chase."

8. Kirkwood to Camp, October 9, 1919; *Buffalo Times-Herald*, November 14, 1924.

9. *Campaigning with Crook*, pp. 128–29.

10. Mills, "Notes by Anson Mills"; McGillycuddy, *McGillycuddy, Agent,* p. 61; "Slim Buttes Battlefield," p. 52; *Chicago Times*, September 21, 1876.

11. Schuyler in Crook, *Autobiography*, pp. 208–9.

12. *Ibid.*, p. 209.

13. Clements, "Medical Report," p. 14; Capron, "Indian Border War of 1876," p. 499; Spring, "Dr. McGillycuddy's Diary," p. 292; Finerty, *War-Path and Bivouac*, pp. 199–200.

14. Bourke, "Diary," 6:895.

15. Schuyler in Crook, *Autobiography*, pp. 209–10; Price, *Across the Continent*, p. 164; *Record of Engagements*, p. 61. The soldier killed was Private Cyrus B. Milner of Company A. "Carr's Report," p. 512. On September 15 his "scalped and mutilated remains" were brought to Crook's camp, where they were "decently interred." Schwatka, in *Daily Inter-Ocean*, October 4, 1876.

16. King, *Campaigning with Crook*, pp. 130–31; Bourke, "Diary," 6:893, 895–97; Price, *Across the Continent*, p. 164; Schuyler in Crook, *Autobiography*, p. 209; Finerty, *War-Path and Bivouac*, pp. 201–2.

17. Flynn, "Journal," p. 67. "Weary and broken down," wrote Schwatka, "many a man slept that awful night, as if he was but a drunkard in the slums of a city, prostrate on the wet ground." *Daily Inter-Ocean*, October 4, 1876.

18. "Medical Report," p. 18.

19. *On the Border with Crook*, p. 379.

20. Mills, *My Story*, p. 168; Flynn, "Journal," p. 68; Finerty, *War-Path and Bivouac*, p. 202; "Battle of Slim Buttes by Gen. G. F. Chase"; *Chicago Times*, September 21, 1876.

21. "Diary," 6:900.

22. On September 13 the Deadwood City Council voted to extend "the hospitalities of the . . . City" to General Crook and solicit "a personal visit" from him. Mayor E. B. Farnum and two council members were appointed to meet Crook and "aid in securing his presence." National Archives, Record Group 393, Department of Dakota, LS, p. 44.

23. Finerty, *War-Path and Bivouac*, p. 202. These pictures repose in the Morrow Collection in the W. H. Over Museum, University of South Dakota, Vermillion. See Wesley R. Hurt and William R. Loss, *Frontier Photographer: Stanley J. Morrow's Dakota Years*, pp. 105–107.

24. *Cincinnati Commercial*, September 19, 1876.

25. *Daily Inter-Ocean*, October 11, 1876.

26. "Bubb interview, 1915." Captain Burt gave a lively account of this episode, writing that Jack Crawford "gained permission from Gen. Merritt to go to Fort Laramie 'on business,' with his precious dispatches [from Davenport] carefully [hidden] beneath his buckskin shirt. Frank Gruard [*sic*], a guide, was entrusted with despatches secretly by other correspondents, and it was thought that both he and Crawford were going to Crook City and Deadwood with the advance of the troops. Crawford was aware that Gruard had despatches [and] had been supplied liberally with money by the correspondents to pay any expense that might arise, even to the purchase of fresh horses at every stage of the ride, while he was without funds with the exception of an old fifty cents fractional currency 'shinplaster' which he found in the pocket of a pair of old overalls Davenport had given him the day before, his buckskin pants standing sorely in need of half soleing. Soon after leaving the main body of troops Crawford quietly dropped away from the detachment and got into a ravine out of sight, and as soon as he could do so unobserved struck the trail and set out on his long ride, determined to earn the $500 offered. While resting at Custer City for an hour Gruard overtook him and asked Crawford to make an agreement with him that both men should rest there for the night and start together next morning. Feeling every confidence in his ability to beat his rival in a square race, Jack agreed to this, and being greatly worn out laid down to take a sleep. He felt anxious and worried fearing treachery on the part of the half breed, and in the night went to his room. Gruard was in bed, but not yet satisfied Crawford made some inquiries and learned that Gruard had hired one of his (Crawford's) old scouts then at Custer to take the despatches, had put him on a fresh horse and started him on the trail three hours before. In haste he went to the stable to get his horse and to his dismay found that the great ride of the day had been too much for him, and he had given up the ghost. He used every argument to induce a friend there to let him take a race mare he had to ride to Fort Laramie, but the friend told him he could never get through alive and would not permit him to commit suicide in that manner if he could prevent it. In the early hours of morning Jack went to the friend's stable and stole the mare and set forth, passed his rival somewhere on the trail and beat him and four other relays of couriers into the fort [by] several hours. . . .

"James Gordon Bennett some months later paid Crawford $225 for horses killed and expenses, making $725 he received for making the remarkable ride." "Account of Slim Buttes."

27. Recalled Keyes: "It is doubtful if one of the 2,500 men composing the expedition expected to see me return. The hostiles in large number were in our rear. The chance of success seemed so small I slipped my

ring from my finger and left it with a letter to be sent to my home should I not return." "A Modern Pocahontas," *Recreation* 10 (January, 1899): 23. This party nearly had a brush with the Indians during the night. The men reached the buried ammunition at about noon the following day and returned to the command without incident. *Ibid.*, pp. 23–24.

28. Bourke, "Diary," 6:910–12; Spring, "Dr. McGillycuddy's Diary," p. 292; Sheridan's Report, p. 446; Hyde, *Spotted Tail's Folk*, p. 227.

29. Telegram, Crook to Sheridan, September 15, 1876, National Archives, Record Group 393, Department of Dakota, LS, p. 38.

30. Adjutant Bourke to Clements, September 15, 1876. National Archives, Record Group 93, Department of Dakota, LS, pp. 37–38.

31. Clements, "Medical Report," p. 21; Bourke, "Diary," 6:924.

32. *War-Path and Bivouac*, p. 207.

33. *New York Times*, October 12, 1876.

34. *Chicago Times*, September 23, 1876. See also Estelline Bennett, *Old Deadwood Days*, pp. 131–32.

35. *Chicago Times*, September 23, 1876.

36. Extracts from "Record of Medical History of Post Medical Department—Camp Robinson," 1874–1879. Ricker tablet 31; Post Return, September, 1876, Fort Laramie, Wyoming.

37. *Milwaukee Sentinel*, October 20, 1876; *Daily Inter-Ocean*, October 11, 1876; "Battle of Slim Buttes by Gen. G. F. Chase"; Howard, "Extracts from a Diary," p. 3; Muster Roll, Company E, Third Cavalry, August 31–October 31, 1876.

38. *Milwaukee Sentinel*, October 20, 1876.

39. *Ibid.*; *Daily Inter-Ocean*, October 11, 1876; Muster Rolls, August 31–October 31, 1876.

40. *Milwaukee Sentinel*, October 20, 1876. Schwatka described Custer City: "In the Augustan period of its history, only a brief year ago, it boasted from 2,000 to 3,000 souls, but the mines of the north have reduced it to one-tenth that number. It is at present 'looming up,' as the inhabitants say, owing to its superior facilities for a winter camp, being nearer to the general base of supplies on the Union Pacific Railroad, and should there be a good supply of people for the hills next year, it may yet see its many deserted buildings again occupied." *Daily Inter-Ocean*, October 11, 1876.

41. Muster Rolls, August 31–October 31, 1876.

42. Price, *Across the Continent*, p. 165; Paul L. Hedren, ed., "Eben Swift's Army Service on the Plains, 1876–1879," *Annals of Wyoming* 50 (Spring, 1978): 145; Muster Rolls, August 31–October 31, 1876; Clements, "Medical Report," p. 21; Howard, "Extracts from a Diary," p. 3.

43. "Crook's Report," September 25, 1876.

44. Quoted in Price, *Across the Continent*, p. 165.

45. Beyer and Keydel, *Deeds of Valor*, 1: 226; *The Medal of Honor of the United States Army*, pp. 226–27.

46. "Mills's Report," pp. 510–11. Some of the Mills's soldiers received certificates of merit for distinguished service at Slim Buttes, entitling them to two dollars extra pay a month for the duration of their military careers. Typical among them was Private John Taylor, Company G, Third Cavalry, who was granted a certificate of merit "for gallantry in action . . . in charging with a small detachment into the center of the enemy under a heavy fire, and bringing out the ponies at the risk of his life." *Official Army Register for 1901*, p. 394.

47. *New York Times*, October 12, 1876; DeLand, "The Sioux Wars," pp. 210–211.

48. *Ellis County Star*, October 12, 1876.

49. *New York Times*, October 12, 1876.

50. *Ellis County Star*, October 12, 1876.

51. Quoted in Anderson, "Family Letters," p. 66.

52. October 28, 1876.

53. September 18, 1876.

54. In Brown and Willard, *Black Hills Trails*, p. 231.

55. *War-Path and Bivouac*, p. 204. From his sickbed in Crook City, Lieutenant Von Luettwitz wrote the following letter to Crook which appeared in the *Army and Navy Journal*, November 4, 1876: "General, I am sorry to leave the army, and especially to be deprived of the pleasure of serving under such an able and energetic officer as yourself. I have been a soldier since my seventeenth year, having been graduated at the Artillery and Engineer school of Berlin. Now it is all over. Your march from Heart River to the Hills showed both your generalship and your duty as a true soldier. Seeing a large Indian trail going south toward your department, you considered it your duty to follow it and protect your wards. You feared neither hardships nor privations, but shared equally with us.

"Nobody can blame you that our campaign was not crowned with complete success. Our forces were too small. The area of country passed over by your command extends from the North Platte to the Yellowstone, and from the Big Horn to the Little Missouri—an area more than twice the size of France. Eight hundred thousand Prussians could not successfully occupy France in 1870. How could two thousand men be expected to control twice as large a country?" Von Luettwitz died March 29, 1887. Heitman, *Historical Register*, I, 989.

56. H. W. Daly, *Manual of Pack Transportation*, pp. 17–18.

57. Finerty, *War-Path and Bivouac*, p. 204; Walter M. Camp, "Address of January 17, 1920," *Winners of the West*, 10 (October 30, 1933).

58. Hyde, *Red Cloud's Folk*, p. 276; Schell, *History of South Dakota*, p. 138.

59. *Report of the Commissioner of Indian Affairs, 1876*, p. 393.

60. Hyde, *Red Cloud's Folk*, pp. 277, 278, 279; Hyde, *Spotted Tail's Folk*, pp. 226–27. Only 40 Indians signed the agreement, out of 2,267 needed to legally comply with the law of 1868. Roger T. Grange, "Fort Robinson, Outpost on the Plains," *Nebraska History* 39 (September, 1958):212.

61. Schell, *History of South Dakota*, p. 138. See also J. M. Lee to Ezra A. Hayt, August 10, 1877, in *Report of the Commissioner of Indian Affairs, 1877*, p. 462.

Epilogue

1. See Appendix D for Camp's account of his search for the battlefield. See also Mills, *My Story*, pp. 168–70; "Slim Buttes Battlefield," p. 47; "Battle of Slim Buttes" (*Cavalry Journal*), pp. 405–407; and Hanson, "History of Harding County," p. 526n.

2. Kirkwood to Camp, September 8 and 13, 1922. Camp Manuscripts, Brigham Young University. Camp to W. C. Brown, March 19, 1925. Papers of the Order of Indian Wars of the United States, U.S. Army Military History Institute, Army War College, Carlisle Barracks, Pennsylvania.

3. Hanson, "History of Harding County," p. 526; Walter M. Camp, "Some of the Indian Battles and Battlefields," in *Proceedings of the Annual Meeting and Dinner of the Order of Indian Wars of the United States, held January Seventeenth Nineteen Hundred and Twenty*, pp. 35–36.

4. Veteran officers of Slim Buttes who supported Miles's recommendation for Mills to receive a Medal of Honor where Major General Samuel S. Sumner, Brigadier General Charles King, Brigadier General William P. Hall, Brigadier General Peter D. Vroom, Colonel C. D. Parkhurst, Lieutenant Colonel Junius L. Powell, and Major H. R. Lemly. Sergeant Kirkwood also supported the application. Lieutenant General Nelson A. Miles to the Adjutant General, July 18, 1921. Denial of the application is in Secretary of War John W. Weeks to Miles, late 1921. Mills Collection, University of Wyoming.

5. Enclosed in Brigadier General Charles Morton to Camp, August 19, 1914. Camp Papers, Ellison Collection.

BIBLIOGRAPHY

Manuscript Materials

Bloomington, Indiana. University of Indiana Library. Manuscripts Division. Robert S. Ellison Collection.

Carlisle Barracks, Pennsylvania. United States Army Military History Institute. Andrew Burt Papers.

―――. E. A. Carr Papers.

―――. Papers of the Order of Indian Wars of the United States.

Crow Agency, Montana. Custer Battlefield National Monument. Accession Records.

―――. [Flynn, Richard.] "Journal of Big Horn and Yellowstone Expedition, 1876." Transcribed copy in the Research Files.

―――. Fred Dustin Collection.

Denver, Colorado, Author's collection. "Diary of Lieutenant John G. Bourke." Transcribed copy furnished by Mark H. Brown.

―――, Denver Public Library. Western History Division. Robert S. Ellison Collection.

El Paso, Texas, Chamber of Commerce. List of items lent by Mrs. Willis B. Shontz for the centennial observance of Fort Bliss, November, 1948.

Laramie, Wyoming. University of Wyoming Library, Western History Research Center. Anson Mills Collection.

Lincoln, Nebraska. Nebraska State Historical Society. Eli S. Ricker Collection.

Provo, Utah. Brigham Young University Library. Manuscripts Division. Walter Mason Camp Manuscripts.

Vermillion, South Dakota. [Keirnes, Helen R.] "Final Days of the Indian Campaign of 1876–1877: Aftermath of the Little Big Horn." Unpublished master's thesis, University of South Dakota, 1969.

Tucson, Arizona. Arizona Historical Society. Glover Collection.

Washington, D.C. National Archives. Record Group 94. Records of the Adjutant General's Department.

――――. Record Group 75. Records of the Bureau of Indian Affairs.

――――. Record Group 393. Records of United States Army Continental Commands.

――――. National Archives Microfilm Publications. Sioux War Papers.

Government Publications

American Military History, 1607–1958. Washington, D.C.: Government Printing Office, 1959.

Daly, H. W. *Manual of Pack Transportation.* Washington, D.C. Government Printing Office, 1910.

Heitman, Francis B., comp. *Historical Register and Dictionary of the United States Army, from its Organization, September 29, 1789, to March 2, 1903.* 2 vols. Washington, D.C.: Government Printing Office, 1903.

Official Army Register for 1901. Washington, D.C.: Adjutant General's Office, 1900.

Record of Engagements with Hostile Indians Within the Military Division of the Missouri from 1868 to 1882. Washington, D.C.: Government Printing Office, 1882.

Report of the Commissioner of Indian Affairs, 1876. Washington, D.C.: Government Printing Office, 1876.

Report of the Commissioner of Indian Affairs, 1877. Washington, D.C.: Government Printing Office, 1878.

Report of the Secretary of War, 1876. Washington, D.C.: Government Printing Office, 1876.

The Medal of Honor of the United States Army. Washington, D.C.: Government Printing Office, 1948.

War Department, Surgeon General's Office. Circular No. 9, "A Report to the Surgeon General of the Transport of Sick and Wounded by Pack Animals," by George A. Otis. Washington, D.C.: Government Printing Office, 1877.

Articles

"The Affair at Slim Buttes." *South Dakota Historical Collections* 6 (1912): 493–590.

Anderson, Harry H. "Charles King's *Campaigning with Crook*: A New and Personal Version Revealed in Family Letters."

Chicago Westerner's Brand Book 32 (January, 1976): 65–67, 70–72.

———. "Cheyennes at the Little Big Horn—A Study of Statistics." *North Dakota Historical Society Quarterly* 27 (Spring, 1960): 3–15.

———. "The Battles of Slim Buttes." *Chicago Westerners' Brand Book* 22 (September, 1965): 49–51, 55–56.

"The Battle of Slim Buttes." *Journal of the United States Cavalry Association* 28 (January, 1918): 399–408.

Brown, W. C., and King, Charles. "Map Showing Many Battlefields of the Indian Wars and the Trail of the Big Horn and Yellowstone Expedition of 1876." Reprint. Fort Collins, Colo.: Old Army Press, n.d.

Camp, Walter M. "Address of January 17, 1920," *Winners of the West,* 10 (October 30, 1933).

———. "Discovery of the Lost Site of the Slim Buttes Battle." *South Dakota Historical Collections* 9 (1918): 55–68.

———. "Some of the Indian Battles and Battlefields." In *Proceedings of the Annual Meeting and Dinner of the Order of Indian Wars of the United States, held January Seventeenth Nineteen Hundred and Twenty.* Washington, D.C. 1920, pp. 19–38.

Capron, Cynthia J. "The Indian Border War of 1876." *Journal of the Illinois State Historical Society* 13 (January, 1921): 476–503.

DeLand, Charles E. "The Sioux Wars." *South Dakota Historical Collections,* 17 (1934): 177–551.

Dobak, William A. "Yellow-Leg Journalists: Enlisted Men as Newspaper Reporters in the Sioux Campaign, 1876." *Journal of the West* 13 (January, 1974): 86–112.

Granger, Roger T. "Fort Robinson, Outpost on the Plains." *Nebraska History* 39 (September, 1958): 191–239.

Greene, Jerome A. "The Crawford Affair: International Implications of the Geronimo Campaign." *Journal of the West* 11 (January, 1972): 143–53.

Hanson, Myrle George. "A History of Harding County, South Dakota, to 1925." *South Dakota Historical Collections* 21 (1942): 515–65.

Hedren, Paul L. "Captain Charles King at Sunset Pass." *Journal of Arizona History* 17 (Autumn, 1976): 253–64.

———, ed. "Eben Swift's Army Service on the Plains, 1876–1879." *Annals of Wyoming* 50 (Spring, 1978): 141–55.

182   SLIM BUTTES, 1876

Helvie, William E. Letter. *Winners of the West*, 5 (March 30, 1928).

Howard, George S. "Extracts from a Diary." *Winners of the West* 14 (February, 1937):3.

Keyes, Edward L. "A Modern Pocahontas." *Recreation* 10 (January, 1899):23–24.

King, Charles. "Memories of a Busy Life," *Wisconsin Magazine of History* 5 (March, 1922):214–43.

King, James T. "General Crook at Camp Cloud Peak: 'I Am at a Loss What to Do.'" *Journal of the West* 11 (January, 1972):114–27.

———. "Needed: A Re-Evaluation of General George Crook." *Nebraska History* 45 (September, 1964):223–35.

McClernand, Edward J. "The Second Regiment of Cavalry." *Journal of the Military Institution of the United States* 13 (1892):629–42.

Mears, David T. "Campaigning Against Crazy Horse." *Proceedings and Collections of the Nebraska State Historical Society* 15 (1907):68–77.

"The Slim Buttes Battlefield." *South Dakota Historical Collections* 9 (1918):47–54.

Spooner, Harry W. [Jefferson, H. W.] Letter to Lester Wallace, October 13, 1886. *Journal of the United States Cavalry Association* 20 (1909–10):1235.

Spring, Agnes Wright, ed. "Dr. McGillycuddy's Diary." *Denver Westerners' Brand Book, 1953.* Boulder, Colo.: Johnson Company, 1954.

Taunton, Francis B. "Army Failures Against the Sioux in 1876." *English Westerners' Brand Book* 5 (April, 1963):1–12.

Turcheneske, John A., Jr. "John G. Bourke: Troubled Scientist." *Journal of Arizona History* 20 (Autumn, 1979):323–44.

Newspapers

Army and Navy Journal. 1876.
Belle Fourche Bee (South Dakota). 1917.
Brownsville Herald, (Texas). 1931.
Buffalo Times-Herald (South Dakota). 1924.
Chicago Times. 1876.
Chicago Tribune. 1876.
Cincinnati Commercial. 1876.
Daily Inter-Ocean (Chicago). 1876.
Daily Rocky Mountain (Denver). 1876.

Ellis County Star (Hays, Kans.). 1876.
Inyo Independent (Independence, Calif.). 1871.
Milwaukee Sentinel. 1876.
New-York Daily Herald. 1876.
New York Times. 1876.

Bulletins

The Wi-iyohi: Monthly Bulletin of the South Dakota State Historical Society 2 (July 1, 1948).
The Wi-iyohi: Monthly Bulletin of the South Dakota State Historical Society 20 (September 1, 1966).

Books

Bennett, Estelline. *Old Deadwood Days.* London: Charles Scribner's Sons, 1935.
Bell, William Gardner. *John Gregory Bourke: A Soldier-Scientist on the Frontier.* Washington, D.C.: Potomac Corral of the Westerners, 1978.
Beyer, W. F., and Keydel, O. F., eds. *Deeds of Valor.* 2 vols. Detroit: Perrien Kydel, 1907.
Boatner, Mark M., III. *The Civil War Dictionary.* New York: David McKay, 1959.
Bourke, John G. *On the Border with Crook.* New York: Charles Scribner's Sons, 1891.
Brady, Cyrus Townsend. *Indian Fights and Fighters.* New York: Doubleday and Co., 1904.
Brown, Jesse, and Willard, A. M. *The Black Hills Trails.* Rapid City, S. Dak.: Rapid City Journal Co., 1924.
Brown, Mark H. *The Plainsmen of the Yellowstone: A History of the Yellowstone Basin.* New York: G. P. Putnam's Sons, 1961.
Camp, Walter M. *Custer in '76: Walter Camp's Notes on the Custer Fight.* Edited by Kenneth Hammer. Provo, Utah: Brigham Young University Press, 1976.
Crook, George. *General George Crook: His Autobiography.* Edited by Martin F. Schmitt. Norman: University of Oklahoma Press, 1960.
DeBarthe, Joe. *Life and Adventures of Frank Grouard.* Edited by Edgar I. Stewart. Norman: University of Oklahoma Press, 1958.
Eastman, Charles. *Indian Heroes and Great Chieftains.* Boston: Little, Brown, and Co., 1929.
Emmitt, Robert. *The Last War Trail: The Utes and the Settle-

ment of Colorado. Norman: University of Oklahoma Press, 1954.

Finerty, John F. *War-Path and Bivouac; or the Conquest of the Sioux.* Norman: University of Oklahoma Press, 1961.

Forsyth, George A. *The Story of the Soldier.* New York: Brampton Society, 1908.

Fritz, Henry E. *The Movement for Indian Assimilation, 1860–1890.* Philadelphia: University of Pennsylvania Press, 1963.

Gibbon, John. *Gibbon on the Sioux Campaign of 1876.* Bellevue, Nebr.: Old Army Press, 1970.

Graham, William A., ed. *The Custer Myth.* Harrisburg: Stackpole Co., 1953.

Gray, John S. *Centennial Campaign: The Sioux War of 1876.* Fort Collins, Colo.: Old Army Press, 1976.

Hamilton, W. T. *My Sixty Years on the Plains: Trapping, Trading, and Indian Fighting.* Norman: University of Oklahoma Press, 1960.

Hanson, Joseph Mills. *The Conquest of the Missouri; Being the Story of the Life and Exploits of Captain Grant Marsh.* New York: Murray Hill Books, 1946.

Harper's Encyclopaedia of United States History from 458 A.D. to 1902. 10 vols. New York: Harper and Brothers, 1902.

Hughes, Richard B. *Pioneer Years in the Black Hills.* Edited by Agnes Wright Spring. Glendale, Calif.: Arthur H. Clark Co., 1957.

Hurt, Wesley R., and Loss, William R. *Frontier Photographer: Stanley J. Morrow's Dakota Years.* Lincoln: University of Nebraska Press, 1956.

Hutchins, James S. *Boots and Saddles at the Little Bighorn.* Fort Collins, Colo.: Old Army Press, 1976.

Hyde, George E. *Red Cloud's Folk: A History of the Oglala Sioux Indians.* Norman: University of Oklahoma Press, 1937.

———. *Spotted Tail's Folk: A History of the Brulé Sioux.* Norman: University of Oklahoma Press, 1961.

King, Charles. *Campaigning with Crook.* Norman: University of Oklahoma Press, 1964.

King, James T. *War Eagle: A Life of General E. A. Carr.* Lincoln: University of Nebraska Press, 1963.

Knight, Oliver. *Following the Indian Wars: The Story of the Newspaper Correspondents Among the Indian Campaigners.* Norman: University of Oklahoma Press, 1960.

————. *Life and Manners in the Frontier Army*. Norman: University of Oklahoma Press, 1978.

Laubin, Reginald and Gladys. *The Indian Tipi: Its History, Construction, and Use*. Norman: University of Oklahoma Press, 1957.

Marquis, Thomas B. *Wooden Leg: A Warrior Who Fought Custer*. Lincoln: University of Nebraska Press, 1957.

Mattes, Merrill J. *Indians, Infants, and Infantry: Andrew and Elizabeth Burt on the Frontier*. Denver: Old West Publishing Co., 1960.

McGillycuddy, Julia B. *McGillycuddy, Agent: A Biography of Dr. Valentine T. McGillycuddy*. Palo Alto, Calif.: Stanford University Press, 1941.

Mills, Anson. *My Story*. Edited by C. H. Claudy. Washington, D.C.: Byron S. Adams, 1921.

Mills, William W. *Forty Years at El Paso*. Edited by Rex W. Strickland. El Paso, Texas: Carl Hertzog, 1962.

Neihardt, John G. *Black Elk Speaks: Being the Life Story of a Holy Man of the Oglala Sioux*. Lincoln: University of Nebraska Press, 1961.

Price, George F., comp. *Across the Continent with the Fifth Cavalry*. New York: Antiquarian Press, 1959.

Richardson, James D., ed. *A Compilation of the Messages and Papers of the Presidents, 1789-1908*. 11 vols. Washington, D.C.: Bureau of National Literature and Art, 1909.

Rickey, Don, Jr. *War in the West: The Indian Campaigns*. Billings, Mont.: Custer Battlefield Historical and Museum Association, 1956.

Rodenbough, Theophilus F. *Uncle Sam's Medal of Honor*. New York: G. P. Putnam's Sons, 1886.

Rosen, Peter. *Pa-Ha-Sa-Pah; or, the Black Hills of South Dakota*. St. Louis: Nixon-Jones Printing Co., 1895.

Russell, Don. *The Lives and Legends of Buffalo Bill*. Norman: University of Oklahoma Press, 1960.

Sandoz, Mari. *Crazy Horse, the Strange Man of the Oglalas*. New York: Hastings House, 1942.

Schell, Herbert S. *History of South Dakota*. Lincoln: University of Nebraska Press, 1961.

Spring, Agnes Wright. *The Cheyenne and Black Hills Stage and Express Routes*. Lincoln: University of Nebraska Press, 1948.

Stewart, Edgar I. *Custer's Luck*. Norman: University of Oklahoma Press, 1955.

Tallent, Annie D. *The Black Hills; or, The Last Hunting Ground of the Dakotahs*. St. Louis: Nixon-Jones Printing Co., 1899.

Trenholm, Virginia Cole, and Carley, Maurine. *The Shoshonis: Sentinels of the Rockies*. Norman: University of Oklahoma Press, 1964.

Utley, Robert M. *Frontier Regulars: The United States Army and the Indian, 1866–1890*. New York: Macmillan Co., 1973.

———. *Frontiersmen in Blue: The United States Army and the Indian, 1848–1865*. New York: Macmillan Co., 1967.

Vaughn, J. W. *Indian Fights: New Facts on Seven Encounters*. Norman: University of Oklahoma Press, 1966.

———. *The Reynolds Campaign on Powder River*. Norman: University of Oklahoma Press, 1961.

———. *With Crook at the Rosebud*. Harrisburg: Stackpole Co., 1956.

Vestal, Stanley. *New Sources of Indian History*. Norman: University of Oklahoma Press, 1934.

———. *Sitting Bull, Champion of the Sioux*. Norman: University of Oklahoma Press, 1957.

———. *Warpath and Council Fire: The Plains Indians' Struggle for Survival in War and in Diplomacy*. New York: Random House, 1948.

Weigley, Russell F. *History of the United States Army*. New York: Macmillan Co., 1967.

———. *The American Way of War: A History of United States Military Strategy and Policy*. New York: Macmillan Co., 1973.

INDEX

187